PRATIQUE DES LANGUES

ANGLAIS de A à Z

EXERCICES 1er NIVEAU

Claude VOLLAIRE

HATIER

AVANT-PROPOS

Ce cahier d'exercices a été conçu pour ceux qui souhaitent vérifier leurs connaissances grammaticales en s'entraînant à manier des structures. Il est la mise en application des règles, remarques et conseils de la *Pratique de l'anglais de A à Z* de M. Swan et F. Houdart (Hatier Paris, Novembre 1983).

Les exercices ont été regroupés en courtes séquences, non plus par ordre alphabétique, mais dans l'ordre du programme officiel, plus « thématique ». Cela permet donc de faire une « synthèse » des connaissances acquises.

Les chapitres et exercices sont accompagnés de références constantes à la *Pratique de l'anglais de A à Z* de manière à pouvoir s'y reporter (par exemple : **"Be" ou "Have"? A à Z : 32-144**).

Les exercices correspondent au programme grammatical et lexical des classes de 4e et 3e des Collèges.

La forme d'entraînement est assez variée : questionnaires à choix multiples, exercices lacunaires (phrases ou textes à compléter), transformations, substitutions, etc. Les exemples donnés et les phrases choisies ajoutent à la variété, tout en restant suffisamment simples pour ne pas dérouter l'utilisateur.

Ce cahier comporte bien des exercices et non des « pièges ». Il s'agit avant tout de s'entraîner. Ainsi, les explications données sont claires et un exemple montre à chaque fois comment on doit procéder. Tous les exercices proposés sont corrigés.

Certes, il est plaisant d'adoucir un peu la rigueur du travail par quelques extraits de B.D. célèbres et par de nombreux "cartoons", mais il est aussi utile de s'apercevoir que les tournures étudiées n'existent pas que dans les « grammaires » ! Le choix des illustrations va dans ce sens.

Conseils d'utilisation :

Il est préférable de consulter la *Pratique de l'anglais de A à Z* AVANT de faire un exercice portant sur un point particulier. Les renvois sont clairement indiqués en début de chapitre et d'exercice.

Lorsque l'exercice est terminé, que le corrigé a été consulté, il faut « s'auto-évaluer » sans aucune complaisance. Si la moindre erreur a été commise, il ne faut surtout pas hésiter à consulter de nouveau la *Pratique de l'anglais de A à Z.*

On ne peut considérer une règle comme « acquise » que lorsqu'on ne se trompe plus et qu'on n'hésite plus ! Il est donc souhaitable de refaire les exercices périodiquement pour s'assurer que tout va toujours bien.

Souhaitons que ce cahier d'exercices soit pour vous un outil de travail efficace et agréable.

C.V.

 ISBN 2-218-**01945**-0.

SOMMAIRE

LES AUXILIAIRES "BE", "HAVE" & "DO"

"BE" ou "HAVE" — p. 4
Réponses courtes — p. 5
Reprise avec "DO" — p. 6
"DO", auxiliaire opérateur — p. 6
"DO" & la forme d'insistance — p. 7

LES AUXILIAIRES MODAUX

Can, could & be able to: la capacité — p. 8
Can, could, may & be allowed to: la permission — p. 9
Must, have to, needn't & mustn't: la nécessité — p. 11
Should & ought to: le conseil, l'obligation morale — p. 12
May, might, could & must: l'éventualité — p. 13
Should & would — p. 15

FORMES NÉGATIVES ET INTERROGATIVES

Les formes négatives — p. 19
Les formes interrogatives — p. 21

LE PRÉSENT

Le présent simple — p. 24
Le présent progressif — p. 26
Présent simple ou présent progressif ? — p. 27

LE PRÉTÉRIT

Le prétérit simple — p. 28
Le prétérit progressif — p. 30
Prétérit simple ou progressif — p. 31

LE "PRESENT PERFECT"

Le "present perfect" simple — p. 32
Le "present perfect"progressif — p. 35
Let — p. 44

LE FUTUR

Will & shall — p. 46
Going to — p. 47
Le futur antérieur — p. 48
Le futur et les subordonnées de temps — p. 49

LE PASSIF

Emploi et formation — p. 50
Le passif de "give", "send", "show", etc. — p. 52

LA FORME FRÉQUENTATIVE

Used to — p. 55
"Used to" ou "be used to +ing" ? — p. 56
"Would" fréquentatif — p. 56

LE PLURIEL DES NOMS

Dénombrables et indénombrables — p. 58
Formation du pluriel — p. 59

LE GÉNITIF

Le cas possessif — p. 62
Le cas possessif « incomplet » — p. 63
Le « double possessif » — p. 63
La traduction de « chez » — p. 64

L'ADJECTIF

Les adjectifs qualificatifs — p. 66
Les adjectifs interrogatifs — p. 71
Les adjectifs possessifs — p. 72
Les adjectifs numéraux — p. 72

LES PRONOMS

Les pronoms personnels — p. 74
Les pronoms réfléchis — p. 75
Les pronoms possessifs — p. 76
Les pronoms interrogatifs — p. 77
Le pronom "one" comme substitut du nom — p. 77

LES ARTICLES

L'article indéfini "A/AN" — p. 78
L'article défini "THE" — p. 79
"A/AN", "THE" ou ø ? — p. 79

LES INDÉFINIS DE QUANTITÉ

Some, any, no, not any — p. 80
Les composés de "some", "any", "no" — p. 81
"Much" ou "many" ? — p. 81
Little, a little, few, a few — p. 82
"All", "each", "every" et ses composés — p. 82
Enough — p. 83

LE DIALOGUE

Réponses courtes — p. 84
Question tags — p. 85
« Moi aussi/moi non plus » — p. 86
Reprises avec "so" — p. 87

LA SUBORDINATION

Pronoms et adverbes relatifs — p. 88
Conjonctions — p. 91

L'INTERROGATION & L'EXCLAMATION

L'interrogation — p. 94
L'exclamation — p. 96

L'INFINITIF & LA FORME EN "-ING"

L'infinitif — p. 98
La forme en "-ing" — p. 101

L'ORDRE DES MOTS DANS LA PHRASE

La place des adverbes — p. 104
La place des compléments — p. 106

PRÉPOSITIONS & PARTICULES

Les prépositions — p. 108
Les particules — p. 110

CORRIGÉS D'EXERCICES — p. 112

INDEX — p. 125

LES AUXILIAIRES "BE", "HAVE" & "DO".

A à Z
41 - 42 - 86 - 87 - 88 - 143 - 144 - 210 - 223 - 271 - 342 A

"BE" OU "HAVE" ? *A à Z : 42 - 144*

1 ***Complétez les phrases suivantes avec AM, IS, ARE, HAS, ou HAVE selon le cas.***

1. It ....'s...... lunchtime ;
Bill and I ....are.... very hungry.

2. Tom, this ...is..... my brother Robert who ...has... just arrived from London.

3. Bob Hawkins ...has... two sisters :
Ann ...is..... 13 and Fiona ...is.... 16.

4. They ..are.... going to France next summer.

5. Excuse me, ..are.... your parents in ?
I ...have... a parcel for them.

6. Come in, Peter ! The door ....is..... open.

"Have you seen Barney?... Barney is a bird dog..."

7. ..Have... you ever been to Scotland, Jenny ? No, I ..have.. never been there.

8. What ...is...... she like ? She ....is.... tall, her hair ....is.... very dark and she ...has... blue eyes.

2 ***Complétez le paragraphe suivant avec WAS, WERE ou HAD, selon le cas.***

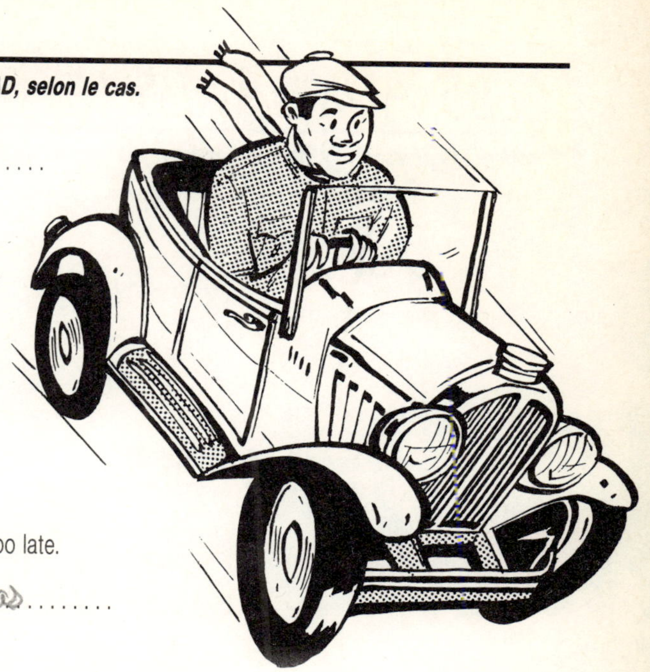

When Grandpa ...was...... young, he ...Had......
a big red car. One day, he ..was.......
driving in the country when his attention ..was.......
drawn to a cow running
in a field. He ....had...... not seen
that two young ladies ...were......
riding their bicycles a few yards ahead of
his car ! When he saw them, it ..was....... almost too late.
He managed to avoid them. One of the young ladies ..was........
frightened and fell off her bicycle.
Grandpa stopped his car and helped her. She ...was....... very pretty. Her name ...was...... Sarah.
You know her. She ....had...... here yesterday. She is my grandmother!

RÉPONSES COURTES

A à Z : 306

3 ***Donnez une réponse courte à chacune des questions du détective.***

Ex. : Do you like music? (Yes) → ***Yes I do.***

1. Do you know Bob Hawkins ? *(No)* ..No, I don't..........
2. Are you sure ? *(Yes)* ..Yes..I'm..............
3. Is John Kelly your friend? *(Yes)* ..Yes, he is.....
4. Have you seen him recently? *(Yes)* ..Yes..I have.
5. Did you see him yesterday? *(Yes)* ..Yes. I did.....
6. Look at this photo. Was this man with him? *(Yes)* ..Yes. He was
7. Had you seen him before? *(No)* ..No., I hadn't.......
8. Were they nervous? *(No)* ..No..they weren't..............

REPRISE AVEC "DO" *A à Z : 88*

4 ***Dans les phrases suivantes, évitez les répétitions à l'aide de DO, DOES ou DID.***

Ex. : Bob never goes to the cinema but I often ***do.***

1. They stayed at the same hotel as we . . . .
2. Mary arrived later than I . . . .
3. I like playing cards and I am sure she . . . .
4. Bob swims much better than you . . . .
5. Ann never wears green but her sister always . . . .
6. It is not very difficult : do as they . . . .
7. We were frightened and Tom ran as fast as I . . . .
8. She speaks German and I think her parents . . . . . .too

"DO", AUXILIAIRE OPÉRATEUR *A à Z : 311 - 318*

5 ***Transformez les affirmations suivantes en questions, puis en déclarations négatives à l'aide de DO, DOES ou DID.***

Ex. : Ken likes playing football. → ***Does*** *Ken* ***like*** *playing football?*
→ *Ken* ***does not*** / ***doesn't like*** *playing football.*

1. They bought this big house . . . . ?

. . . .

2. Mary lives in Manchester . . . . ?

. . . .

3. They have cornflakes for breakfast . . . . ?

. . . .

4. Bill went to school yesterday . . . . ?

. . . .

5. Mr Johnson works in London . . . . ?

. . . .

"DO" & LA FORME D'INSISTANCE

A à Z : 87

6 ***Marquez l'insistance (ou le contraste) en utilisant DO, DOES ou DID pour transformer les phrases suivantes.***

*Ex. : I like coffee, → I **do like** coffee.*

1. Jennifer looked sad, ...

2. I love swimming in the sea ....

3. Bob wants to go now! ....

4. That's exactly what he said ....

5. Please, sit down! ....

6. Tell me who she is ....

7. He promised me not to repeat it ....
....

8. You didn't read that book, I read it ....
....

9. My mother plays the piano ....
....

10. I think you should write to him
....
....
....

LES AUXILIAIRES MODAUX.

A à Z
44 - 45 - 57
58 - 74 - 198
199 - 203 - 207
208 - 209 - 239
274 - 285

"Straight ahead. You can't miss it."

CAN, COULD & BE ABLE TO: LA CAPACITÉ

A à Z : 57 - 44

7 ***Complétez les phrases suivantes avec CAN, CAN'T, COULD ou COULDN'T selon le sens.***

*Ex. : It's too dark, I ... see a thing, → I **can't** see a thing.*

1. My dog is too old ; he .... run any more.
2. Sherlock Holmes was a good musician ; he .... play the violin very well.
3. The door is locked and we .... go out!
4. The box was too heavy and Peter .... lift it.
5. Look! Mary .... swim very well.
6. That dress was not very expensive so Sarah .... buy it.
7. I called them but they .... hear me.
8. John .... speak German, Spanish and French!

8 ***Utilisez BE ABLE TO pour répondre aux questions suivantes.***

*Ex. : Did you see her yesterday? Yes... → Yes I **was able** to see her yesterday.*

1. Will you come to my birthday party? No, we ....
2. Did you meet Mr Smith this morning? Yes, I ....
3. Has Bob done his homework! Yes ....
4. Will they go to Scotland next summer? No, ...
5. Did she answer the question? Yes, ...
6. Do you think he will open the door? No, ...
7. Do they speak Italian? No, ...
8. Did he pay for the dinner? Yes, ...

CAN, COULD, MAY & BE ALLOWED TO: LA PERMISSION

A à Z : 45 - 58

"Miss Ellis, could you come in here and pass me my coffee?"

9 ***A l'aide des éléments suivants, demandez une permission familière avec CAN, puis un peu plus polie avec COULD.***

*Ex. : have some more soup (I). → **Can I have** some more soup please?*
*→ **Could I have** some more soup, please?*

1. borrow your pen *(I)* ....
....
2. watch TV tonight *(we)* ....
....
3. tell me the way to the Post Office *(you)* ....
....
4. speak to Tom *(I)* ....
....
5. lend me 50p *(you)* ....
....

6. use your telephone *(I)* ....

....

7. come with us to the cinema *(John)* ....

....

8. pass me the salt *(you)* ....

....

10 ***Remplacer les verbes ou expressions en capitales par BE ALLOWED TO au temps et à la forme qui conviennent.***

Ex. : They CAN leave now. → They ***are allowed to*** *leave now.*

1. The teacher said that we COULD NOT use a dictionary ....

....

2. You MUSTN'T park your car here ....

....

3. Do you think Peter will BE GIVEN PERMISSION TO go fishing? ....

....

4. We CAN play football in the garden ....

....

5. They MUSTN'T enter this room ....

....

6. I WAS NOT GIVEN PERMISSION TO come back after midnight ....

....

7. You CAN'T sit in this armchair ....

....

8. It's four o'clock. We MAY go home now ....

....

"I must admit, I've been to better poolside parties."

MUST, HAVE TO, NEEDN'T & MUSTN'T: LA NÉCESSITÉ

A à Z : 207 - 209

11 ***Regardez les panneaux routiers et commentez chacun d'entre eux par une phrase contenant MUST ou MUSTN'T.***

*Ex. : No right turn → **You/We mustn't turn right.***

1. Keep left  ....

 2. No waiting ....

3. No cycling  ....

 4. Ahead only ....

5. Give way to traffic on major road 

....

 6. Turn left ....

7. Stop and Give Way 

....

 8. No left turn ....

12 ***Complétez les phrases suivantes à l'aide de HAVE TO (au temps et à la forme qui conviennent) pour exprimer la nécessité (l'obligation) ou son absence.***

Ex. : I .... get up early every morning at present,
*→ **I have to** get up...*
It wasn't late and we .... hurry
*→ ... **we didn't have to hurry.***

1. Helen can't see very well. She .... wear glasses all the time.
2. .... you .... leave now?
3. Our father took us in his car so we .... walk.
4. We were late and we .... run.
5. My car is broken and so we .... take the bus tomorrow.
6. We .... go to school on Sundays.
7 .... you .... finish your work tonight?
8. I was so tired that I .... go to bed early.

13 ***Chacune des phrases suivantes exprime une obligation ou une nécessité. Dites le contraire avec NEEDN'T.***

*Ex. : You must answer immediately → You **needn't answer** immediately.*

1. They have to be there before eight o'clock ....
2. You must call him 'Sir' ....
3. They have to ask my permission to go to the cinema ....
4. Bill has to take his car ....
5. It's necessary for them to speak German to work for that company ....
6. You have to write to us every day ....
7. Sheila has to do her homework now ....
8. You've got to come back tomorrow ....

SHOULD & OUGHT TO: LE CONSEIL, L'OBLIGATION

A à Z : 285 - 239

"You shouldn't stay in the sun more than twenty minutes on the first day, otherwise your bathing costume might fade..."

14 ***Transformez les phrases suivantes avec SHOULD ou SHOULDN'T.***

*Ex. : Don't drink beer. → You **shouldn't drink** beer.*
*Speak louder. → You **should speak** louder.*

1. Take your coat in case it rains ....
2. Learn your lesson ....
3. Don't walk so fast ....
4. Don't use a dictionary ....
5. Don't laugh at your neighbour ....
6. Send a postcard to your parents ....
7. Don't tell her that you know ....
8. Stop talking to your friend ....

15 ***Donnez des conseils en utilisant SHOULD.***

Ex. : Why don't you take the bus? → *You **should take** the bus.*

1. Why don't we park here?

....

2. Why don't you cut the grass?

....

3. Why doesn't he give them a ring from time to time?

....

4. Why don't they stop driving so fast?

....

5. Why doesn't Mary help her sister with her homework?

....

6. Why aren't they more careful?

....

7. Why don't they tell the truth?

....

8. He looks very tired, Why doesn't he send for a doctor?

....

16 ***Donnez des conseils, exprimez des obligations avec OUGHT TO ou OUGHTN'T TO.***

Ex. : Peter doesn't see very well (wear glasses). → *Peter **ought to wear** glasses.*

1. Bob has put on weight *(not eat cakes)* ....
2. I don't feel well *(see a doctor)* ....
3. You will be late *(leave at once)* ....
4. She has a headache *(turn down the radio)* ....
5. I have a bad tooth *(not eat sweets)* ....
6. Jim hasn't done anything yet *(do his exercise now)* ....
7. We have never been abroad *(visit Paris)* ....
8. Smoking is dangerous for your health *(not be allowed)* ....

MAY, MIGHT, COULD & MUST: L'ÉVENTUALITÉ

A à Z : 198 - 199
207 - 208

17 ***Utilisez MAY ou MIGHT dans les phrases suivantes en les transformant comme dans l'exemple ci-dessous.***

Ex. : Perhaps Mary will be late. → *Mary **may be** late.*
Perhaps they'd go out tonight → *They might go out tonight.*

1. Perhaps you'll see him if you go now.

....

2. Don't eat this mushroom, perhaps it is dangerous.

....

3. Drive carefully. Perhaps you'd have an accident if you don't.

....

4. Give him a ring ; perhaps he's at home now? ....

....

5. If we offered him a meal, perhaps Jimmy would come ....

....

6. I think you should buy now. Perhaps prices will go up ....

....

7. If we arrived early, perhaps we'd get good seats ..

....

....

8. Goodbye! Perhaps I 'd never see you again ......

....

....

"Good God, Elizabeth, I think we may be a mirage."

18 ***Complétez le dialogue suivant par des tournures avec COULD de manière à exprimer une éventualité ou une suggestion.***

*Ex.: Tom: I don't like walking. / Richard: (*take the *bus)* → *You* ***could take*** *the bus, couldn't you?*

1. Tom: I really hate writing letters.
Richard: *(send telegrams)* ....
2. Tom: My parents don't like telegrams at all.
Richard: *(give them a ring)* ....
3. Tom: You're right. They haven't heard from me for three months.
Richard: *(visit them next weekend)* ....
4. Tom: That's a good idea. They'll be surprised.
Richard: *(call them right now)* ....
5. Tom: All right, but ... I haven't got a telephone!
Richard: *(go to the post office)* ....
6. Tom: It's very far away and I'll have to take the bus.
Richard: I *(give you a lift)*..

19 ***Transformez les phrases suivantes pour exprimer une très forte probabilité (une déduction) avec MUST.***

Ex. : I'm sure Bill is telling lies, → *Bill* ***must be*** *telling lies.*

1. We're certain the Johnsons are at home ....

....

2. I'm quite sure the train is late ....

....

3. He's not very old. He's in his early thirties ....

....

4. I recognize her, I'm quite sure I've seen her on T.V. ....

....

5. I've just heard a bark. I'm certain it's your dog ....

....

6. John doesn't answer. I think he's asleep ....

....

7. They left in the early morning. I'm sure they have arrived by now ....

....

8. Mary has just sent for a doctor. I'm quite sure she's ill ....

....

"Oh dear, they must be out! All the lights are on."

SHOULD & WOULD

A à Z : 74 - 203
285 - 274 - 348

20 ***Complétez les phrases suivantes à l'aide de SHOULD ou de WOULD, en tenant compte du sens, bien sûr.***

*Ex. : .... you like another cup of tea? → **Would you like...***

1. .... you mind opening the window?

2. This pullover is too big. I .... buy another.

3. What are you doing here at this time of the day? You .... be at school!

4. .... you be very kind and shut the door, please?

5. My exercise is difficult. If Helen was here, she .... help me.

6. If I were very rich, I .... buy a big house in the country.

7. .... you like to go on holiday with them?

8. You . . . . go to bed now, it's late.

9. I know you don't want to do the job but if you . . . . change your mind, let me know!

21 ***Utilisez WOULD dans les phrases suivantes pour décrire une habitude ou la répétition d'une action dans le passé.***

Ex. : My grandparents went to church (on Sundays).
→ *On Sundays my grandparents* ***would go*** *to church.*

1. Grandpa drove his old Ford *(occasionally),* to visit his friends in town.

. . . .

. . . .

2. Grandma stayed at home *(usually),* when Grandpa was visiting his friends.

. . . .

. . . .

3. She made very good cakes *(every Wednesday),* for her grandchildren.

. . . .

. . . .

4. Grandpa played the piano *(every morning),* for two hours, before lunch.

. . . .

. . . .

5. My grandparents watched television *(sometimes),* after dinner.

. . . .

. . . .

6. Grandpa worked in the garden *(every Saturday afternoon),* with the radio turned on very loudly.

. . . .

. . . .

7. Grandma read magazines *(occasionally),* after dinner, instead of watching television.

. . . .

. . . .

8. They went to the supermarket *(once a month),* to buy all their grocery.

. . . .

. . . .

22 ***Exprimez une préférence avec WOULD RATHER en transformant les phrases suivantes.***

Ex. : I don't like walking. I prefer to go by bus.
*→ **I would rather** go by bus.*

1. My father hates taking the bus. He prefers to drive to town.

....

....

2. John doesn't like towns. He prefers to live in the country.

....

....

3. I don't want to play cards. I prefer to watch television.

....

....

4. She doesn't like meat very much. She prefers to have fish.

....

....

5. They don't like handball. They prefer to play football.

....

....

6. We don't like pop music. We prefer to listen to classical music.

....

....

7. I don't like films very much. I prefer to read a good book.

....

....

8. Bill doesn't like beer. He prefers to drink water.

....

....

23 ***A l'aide des éléments suivants, construisez des phrases exprimant une probabilité moyenne avec SHOULD.***

Ex. : You leave now. You arrive there in the evening.
*→ **If you leave now, you should arrive there in the evening.***

1. He listens carefully. He understands everything.

....

2. You take this key. You open that door.

....

3. She phones her parents. They are happy.

....

4. You open that drawer. You find a pair of scissors.

....

5. They look this way. They see the Post Office Tower.

....

6. I insert 50p in the machine. I get a sandwich.

....

FORMES NÉGATIVES ET INTERROGATIVES

A à Z

165 - 210 - 211 - 212 - 232 - 271 - 303 - 304

LES FORMES NÉGATIVES

A à Z : 165 - 210
212 - 232

24 ***Transformez les phrases suivantes en déclarations négatives. Utilisez les contractions.***

*Ex. : He knows my father. → He **doesn't know** my father.*

1. I like playing the piano.

....

2. You should drink coffee.

....

3. She'll be there before 5 o'clock.

....

4. Bob brought his book.

....

5. Little Peter can read very well.

....

6. They were at school yesterday.

....

7. We saw the film last night.

....

8. You have to do your room now.

....

25 ***Ajoutez NEVER aux phrases suivantes pour les rendre négatives.***

*Ex. : She takes the train → She **never** takes the train.*

1. Bob has been abroad.

....

2. I watch T.V. in the evening.

....

3. The shops are closed on Sundays.

....

4. You'll see the church from here.

....

5. We shall go there again.

....

6. I had heard that before.

....

7. He would be late for school.

....

8. They listen to pop music.

....

26 ***Utilisez NEITHER ... NOR pour transformer les affirmations suivantes en négations***

Ex. : She can read and write English.
→ She can ***neither*** *read* ***nor*** *write English.*

1. Patricia and Richard could do the job.

....

2. You and I could have broken that vase.

....

3. My brother sings and dances very well.

....

4. That's good or bad.

....

5. Peter and John will go to your birthday party.

....

6. They should drink beer or cider.

....

7. Ann and Jenny have heard the news on the radio.

....

8. Joe speaks Italian and German.

....

27 ***A l'aide des éléments suivants, construisez des phrases contenant un INFINITIF NÉGATIF.***

Ex. : be late (I hope) → *I hope* ***not to be*** *late.*

1. forget that *(he'll try).*

....

2. repeat it *(they told me).*

....

3. stay here *(the police said).*

....

4. arrive before 8 *(she asked him).*

....

5. open the window *(they'd like her).*

....

6. let them know *(it's better).*

....

7. take the train *(he advised us).*

....

8. follow me *(I told Tom).*

....

LES FORMES INTERROGATIVES

A à Z : 211 - 271
303 - 304 - 346

28

Transformez les affirmations suivantes en questions.

Ex. : John got up early this morning.
*→ **Did John get up** early this morning?*

1. Mary went to the shops yesterday.

....?

2. He'd like to have a look at this photo.

....?

3. Mr Smith will arrive in London this afternoon.

....?

4. Bob drives a black Jaguar.

....?

5. They can speak English.

....?

6. She is going to Birmingham next week.

....?

7. We have to go soon.

....?

8. He had seen them before.

....?

29 ***Posez des questions portant sur les mots en italique.***

Ex. : Jenny is ***at school.*** *→* ***Where is Jenny?***

1. Mary is eating *an orange.*

. . . . ?

2. She went to bed *at 10 in the evening.*

. . . . ?

3. *Peter* was late for work.

. . . . ?

4. They *were watching television.*

. . . . ?

5. This is *the Johnsons'* house.

. . . . ?

6. Her parents will go to Glasgow *by train.*

. . . . ?

7. John is *in the living-room.*

. . . . ?

8. Patricia is running *because she wants to catch the bus.*

. . . . ?

9. We'll have to wait *a few minutes.*

. . . . ?

10. Richard's sister is *twelve years old.*

. . . . ?

"And what do you have to say for yourself?"

30

Mettez les phrases suivantes à la forme interro-négative.

Ex. : He carried my suitcase to the car.
*→ **Didn't he carry** my suitcase to the car?*

1. You can listen to Dick's story.

....?

2. Ann is a hard-working girl.

....?

3. You will go to Bob's birthday party.

....?

4. They enjoyed themselves very much.

....?

5. We could ask your parents to give us a lift.

....?

6. Mrs Smith often goes to Manchester.

....?

7. They have already said it was all right.

....?

8. He would play football with us.

....?

31

Complétez les phrases suivantes avec des « questions-tags ».

*Ex. : Dick likes bacon and eggs .... ? → **doesn't he?***

"Why can't we have wheels like the Palefaces?"

1. It was a nice day, ...?
2. Mary can run very fast, ...?
3. She plays the piano, ...?
4. You've read that magazine, ...?
5. They didn't listen to me, ...?
6. Bill wasn't at school yesterday, ...?
7. He didn't have to do that, ...?
8. Sheila's bought a new dress, ...?
9. They will do the job, ...?
10. He wrote that letter, ...?

LE PRÉSENT

A à Z

210 - 310 à 314 - 316

LE PRÉSENT SIMPLE *A à Z : 311*

"That's another thing I can't stand about him–he never stops complaining."

32 ***Transformez les phrases suivantes en les mettant à la troisième personne du singulier.***

Ex. : They catch the 8 o'clock bus every morning. (She)
→ ***She catches** the 8 o'clock bus every morning.*

1. They want me to arrive early. *(Mr Wilde)*

. . . .

2. You watch TV every evening. *(Richard)*

. . . .

3. We try to understand them. *(He)*

. . . .

4. I kiss my mother every morning. *(She)*

. . . .

5. They wash the floor on Saturdays. *(Bill)*

. . . .

6. I always carry a big umbrella. *(Patricia)*

. . . .

7. We change trains at Bristol. *(He)*

. . . .

8. They give us a lot of work to do. *(The teacher)*

. . . .

33 ***Mettez les phrases suivantes à la forme négative, puis à la forme interrogative.***

Ex. : He enjoys listening to music.
***He doesn't enjoy** listening to music.*
***Does he enjoy** listening to music?*

1. They agree with you . . . .

. . . .

2. Ann lives at the seaside . . . .

. . . .

3. You play tennis at school . . . .

. . . .

4. We study Latin this year . . . .

. . . .

5. Bob has cereal for breakfast . . . .

. . . .

6. That butcher sells excellent meat . . . .

. . . .

7. The Andersons go to the U.S.A. every year . . . .

. . . .

8. John walks to school every day . . . .

. . . .

LE PRÉSENT PROGRESSIF *A à Z : 313 - 310²*

34 ***Mettez les verbes entre parenthèses au présent progressif.***

Ex. : What you (do)*? I* (repair) *my bicycle.*
→ ***What are you doing? I'm repairing my bicycle.***

1. Bill *(drink)* a cup of tea.

....

2. Where you *(go)* this summer?

....

3. Bob *(work)* now? No, he *(not work)*. He *(play)* records.

....

4. Look! Those cars *(go)* very fast.

....

5. Why Ann *(run)?* She *(try)* to catch her bus.

....

6. You *(not tell)* the truth.

....

7. Why you *(carry)* an umbrella? Because it *(rain)*.

....

8. We *(have)* breakfast at 7.00 tomorrow.

....

35 ***Mettez les phrases suivantes au présent progressif SI LE VERBE LE PERMET.***

Ex. : John likes tea. → ***pas de forme progressive***
He goes to the cinema. → ***He is going*** *to the cinema.*

1. I don't understand. What do you mean?

....

2. They play football in the back garden.

....

3. He writes a letter to his parents.

....

4. Do you believe his story?

....

5. My father wants me to be a teacher.

....

6. I wish you a merry Christmas and a happy New Year.

....

7. Which book do you prefer?

....

8. Father works in the garden.

....

PRÉSENT SIMPLE OU PRÉSENT PROGRESSIF ?

A à Z : 316

36 ***Mettez les verbes entre parenthèses au présent qui convient.***

Ex. : Henry never (wear) *a hat.*
→ Henry never ***wears*** *a hat.*

1. Look! John *(put on)* his coat. He *(go)* for a walk.

....

2. I *(go)* to London every day. I *(work)* near Piccadilly Circus.

....

3. What Mary *(do)* now? She *(have)* a bath.

....

4. She *(not like)* dogs. She *(prefer)* cats.

....

5. Bill always *(write)* with his left hand.

....

6. The children *(study)* French this year.

....

7. What he *(do)* to his car now? I *(think)* he *(wash)* it.

....

8. Tom is in his room. He *(do)* his homework.

....

37 ***Choisissez la bonne réponse.***

Ex. : He usually ... water.
a. drink b. drinks c. is drinking.
→ ***la bonne réponse est b.: He usually drinks water.***

1. Take your umbrella; it ...
   a. *rains* b. *is raining* c. *is rain.*
2. The Johnsons always ... at 6 every morning.
   a. *getting up* b. *gets up* c. *get up.*
3. This book ... £ 2.50
   a. *costing* b. *is costing* c. *costs.*
4. Hello, Peter. What ... for?
   a. *do you wait* b. *are you waiting* c. *are you wait.*
5. That film ... to the Odeon next week.
   a. *is coming* b. *comes* c. *does come.*
6. They usually ... the bus to school.
   a. *take* b. *are taking* c. *takes.*
7. My sister ... gardening at all.
   a. *isn't liking* b. *isn't like* c. *doesn't like.*
8. Speaking Chinese ... very difficult to me.
   a. *seems* b. *is seeming* c. *seem.*

LE PRÉTÉRIT

A à Z
318 à 320

LE PRÉTÉRIT SIMPLE *A à Z : 318*

"I wrecked my car, I ran into it with your car."

38 ***Mettez les phrases suivantes au prétérit simple, en consultant éventuellement la liste des verbes irréguliers (A14, p. 298).***

Ex. : I see Peter (a minute ago).
→ *I **saw** Peter a minute ago.*

1. Patricia goes to the cinema *(last night).*

....

2. We take the 8.15 bus *(yesterday morning).*

....

3. John looks very tired *(this morning).*

....

4. Mr Riley drives to London *(last week).*

....

5. I buy lots of records *(last year).*

....

6. The children sing very well *(yesterday afternoon).*

....

7. The park closes at 10.30 *(two days ago).*

....

8. I walk to school *(this morning).*

....

39 ***Mettez les phrases suivantes à la forme interrogative, puis à la forme négative.***

Ex. : She liked that film. → ***Did** she **like** that film?*
→ *She **didn't like** that film.*

1. Tom worked at night ....

....

2. You remembered his phone number ....

....

3. Sheila forgot her English book ....

....

4. They agreed with you ....

....

5. Richard brought his guitar ....

....

6. The children did their room this morning ....

....

7. She had bacon and eggs for her breakfast ....

....

8. They finished work at 7.00 last night ....

....

40 ***Écrivez chacun des verbes dans la colonne qui correspond à la prononciation de sa finale -ed (voir 318[2]).***

I received a letter this morning. – We worked hard. – They played hockey. – He waited for us. – Bob picked a few flowers. – They loved each other. – She looked happy. – I enjoyed that party. – He talked to me. – They wanted to come with us.
– John washed the floor.
– What happened?

[d]	[t]	[id]
....	....	....
....	....	....
....	....	....
....	....	....
....	....	....
....	....	....

LE PRÉTÉRIT PROGRESSIF *A à Z : 320*

41 ***Mettez les phrases suivantes au prétérit progressif.***

Ex. : She didn't look at me.
*→ She **wasn't looking** at me.*

1. It rained very heavily.
....
2. We had a cup of tea in the sitting-room.
....
3. Dick cut the grass in the back garden.
....
4. Mr Smith read a magazine.
....
5. Did they watch television?
....
6. He didn't do his homework.
....
7. Mary played the guitar in her room.
....

42 ***Répondez aux questions de Sherlock Holmes.***

Ex. : What were you doing at 9 yesterday evening? (watch TV)
*→ **I was watching TV.***

1. What were you all doing at 5 this afternoon? *(have tea)* ....
....
....
2. What was Mary doing when the doorbell rang? *(read a book)* ....
....
....

3. What was the man doing when she opened the door? *(call for help)* ....

....

4. What was your neighbour doing when you saw him? *(run away)* ....

....

5. What was the man doing when he died? *(try to tell us a name)* ....

....

6. What were you doing when I arrived? *(wait for the police)* ....

....

7. What was Mary doing when I entered the room? *(look through the window)*

....

8. What was your dog doing in the street? *(follow the neighbour)* ....

....

PRÉTÉRIT SIMPLE OU PROGRESSIF ? *A à Z : 319-320*

43 ***Mettez les verbes entre parenthèses au prétérit qui convient.***

Ex. : John (wait) *for the bus when I* (see) *him.*
→ *John* ***was waiting*** *for the bus when I* ***saw*** *him.*

1. When I *(meet)* her, she *(go)* to the shops.

....

2. When I *(call)* him he *(tell)* me he *(paint)* the front door.

....

3. As I *(come)* to her a policeman *(stop)* me.

....

4. While I *(dig)* in the garden it *(begin)* to rain.

....

5. When they *(leave)* we *(work)* in the kitchen.

....

6. I *(sleep)* very well when the dog *(wake)* me up.

....

7. What you *(do)* when I *(ring)* the doorbell?

....

8. The sun *(shine)* when we *(get up)*.

....

9. He *(try)* to open the door when he suddenly *(remember)* he had no key

....

LE "PRESENT PERFECT"

A à Z
120 - 180 - 321 à 323 - 328

LE "PRESENT PERFECT" SIMPLE

A à Z : 321 - 180
323R.² - 120

44 ***Mettez les verbes entre parenthèses au "present perfect" simple. Au besoin, consultez la liste des verbes irréguliers (A 14 p. 298).***

Ex. : Where you (be)? → *Where* ***have*** *you* ***been?***

1. He *(not pay)* the telephone bill.

2. I *(buy)* a few oranges.

3. She *(not finish)* her homework yet.

4. John *(cut)* the grass?

5. Someone *(steal)* Mary's car!

6. They *(repair)* the road.

7. You *(see)* my keys anywhere?

8. We *(not hear)* from him lately.

45 ***Transformez les phrases suivantes comme dans l'exemple.***

Ex. : He went out not long ago.
→ *He* ***has just gone*** *out.*

1. I saw Patricia a few minutes ago.

2. We asked him for dinner a minute ago.

3. The train left a moment ago.

4. They gave me a ring just now.

5. Richard came back home not long ago.

6. An accident happened a minute ago.

"How long have you had those trousers, Mr Gumthorpe?"

7. She found her car keys a moment ago.

....

....

8. They had breakfast a few minutes ago.

....

....

46 ***Transformez les phrases suivantes comme dans l'exemple ci-dessous.***

Ex. : It last rained two months ago.
*→ It **hasn't rained for** two months.*

1. I last saw them three weeks ago.

....

2. He last drove a car ten years ago!

....

3. They last talked to me three days ago.

....

4. You last wrote to me six months ago.

....

5. We last heard from Bob two years ago.

....

6. She last took the bus months ago.

....

7. I last ate bacon and eggs ages ago!

....

8. He last met Peter a fortnight ago.

....

47 ***Transformez les phrases suivantes comme dans l'exemple ci-dessous.***

Ex. : She last called me at 2 o'clock.
*→ She **hasn't called** me **since** 2 o'clock.*

1. He last read a newspaper last week.

....

2. We last received a letter from them on June 6th.

....

3. John last came here at the beginning of the month.

....

4. Bob last caught a fish when we arrived.

....

5. They last visited London in 1982.

....

6. I last rode a bicycle when I was a boy.

....

7. She last had lunch at a restaurant in March.

. . . .

8. We last drank beer at the beginning of the week.

. . . .

"Have you been waiting long, Sir?"

LE "PRESENT PERFECT" PROGRESSIF

A à Z : 323 - 120

48 ***Mettez les verbes entre parenthèses au "present perfect" progressif.***

Ex. : It (rain) *for three days.*
→ *It* ***has been raining*** *for three days.*

1. How long you *(wait)* for us?

. . . .

2. They *(live)* in Taunton since 1975.

. . . .

3. Richard *(dig)* in the garden all afternoon.

. . . .

4. The telephone *(ring)* for ten minutes!

. . . .

5. He *(drive)* for twenty years.

. . . .

6. She *(wear)* glasses since she was six years old.

....

7. They *(watch)* TV since 6 p.m.

....

8. Baby *(cry)* for one hour!

....

49 ***Transformez les phrases suivantes.***

Ex. : We started walking two hours ago; we're still walking.
*→ We **have been walking** for two hours.*

1. John started sleeping at 10 o'clock; he's still sleeping.

....

2. I started waiting three hours ago; I'm still waiting.

....

3. He started working for us in 1980; he's still working for us.

....

4. We started living in Bristol five years ago; we're still living there.

....

5. She started fishing one hour ago; she's still fishing.

....

6. They started playing chess at 4 p.m.; they're still playing.

....

7. The sun started shining a fortnight ago; it is still shining.

....

8. Bill started reading that book at the beginning of the afternoon; he's still reading it.

....

PRÉTÉRIT OU "PRESENT PERFECT" ?

A à Z : 319 - 321
322 - 323
180 - 328[3]

50 ***Choisissez la réponse qui convient.***

1. We . . . . . John's parents last week.
   a. *have met* b. *met* c. *have been meeting*
2. I . . . . . playing football two years ago.
   a. *started* b. *have started* c. *starting*
3. He . . . . . a cooked breakfast for ages!
   a. *hasn't been having* b. *hasn't had* c. *didn't have*
4. . . . . . the door before leaving the house?
   a. *Did you lock* b. *Were you locking* c. *Have you locked*

5. They . . . . . working at 5 p.m.
   a. *have stopped* b. *stopped* c. *having stopped*
6. Peter . . . . . back from Italy. He looks very well.
   a. *has just come* b. *just came* c. *was just coming*
7. What . . . . . last night?
   a. *have you done* b. *have you been doing* c. *did you do.*
8. They . . . . . abroad because they can't afford it.
   a. *never were* b. *have never been* c. *were never being*
9. Mr Jenkins . . . . . at nine o'clock.
   a. *was arriving* b. *has arrived* c. *arrived.*
10. Yesterday morning we . . . . . very early.
   a. *have got up* b. *got up* c. *having got up*

51 *Mettez les verbes entre parenthèses aux temps qui conviennent.*

Ex. : They (work) *hard yesterday.*
→ *They **worked** hard yesterday.*
I (not see) *Bill Jenkins for ages.*
→ *I **have not seen** Bill Jenkins for ages.*

1. My neighbours just *(buy)* a big red car.

. . . .

2. We never *(be)* in Switzerland.

. . . .

3. Peter and I *(go)* to the cinema last night.

. . . .

4. Patricia *(start)* practising tennis last month.

. . . .

5. We *(leave)* home at 9.00 and *(get)* there by 11.30

. . . .

6. She *(not finish)* her homework yet.

. . . .

7. The Johnsons *(live)* here since January.

. . . .

8. I *(wait)* for a few minutes.

. . . .

9. Last year Jim *(break)* his leg.

. . . .

10. They *(arrive)* at 10.00 this morning.

. . . .

LE "PLUPERFECT"

A à Z
82 - 325 - 326

LE "PLUPERFECT" SIMPLE

A à Z : 82 - 325

52 ***Transformez les phrases suivantes en mettant le verbe au "pluperfect" simple et en ajoutant BEFORE.***

*Ex. : I read that book. → I **had read** that book **before**.*

1. We heard that strange story.

....

2. Mr and Mrs Holden were in Brussels.

....

3. Richard borrowed my bicycle.

....

4. He gave us a little money.

....

5. Sheila had fish and chips.

....

6. Bill drove a big tractor.

....

7. The children brought me flowers.

....

8. I played football with my friends.

....

53 ***Transformez les phrases suivantes selon l'exemple indiqué ci-dessous.***

Ex. : We drove six miles; we saw a village.
*→ We **had driven** six miles when we saw a village.*

1. It started raining; I went out.

....

2. Paul left for France; his friend came to see him.

....

3. Ann had dinner; Peter invited her to go to a restaurant.

....

4. The play began; I arrived at the theatre.

....

5. We read the book; we saw the film.

....

6. John finished his work; they offered to help him.

....

7. They took all the seats; a woman came in with a baby.

....

8. The thieves ran away; we called the police.

....

LE "PLUPERFECT" PROGRESSIF

A à Z : 326

54 ***Mettez les phrases suivantes : a. au "pluperfect" progressif ; b. à la forme interrogative ; c. à la forme négative.***

Ex. : They'd worked in the garden.
*→ They'd **been working** in the garden.*
*→ **Had** they **been working** in the garden?*
*→ They **hadn't been working** in the garden.*

1. I'd looked for a shoe shop the whole morning.

....

....

....

2. She'd driven the car all the way.

....

....

....

3. They'd danced all night.

....

....

....

4. It'd rained all the week.

....

....

....

5. He'd talked on the telephone for twenty minutes.

....

....

....

6. The wind had blown for two days.

....

....

....

7. We'd sung many folk songs.

....

....

....

8. She'd read a magazine for an hour.

....

....

....

PRETERIT, "PRESENT PERFECT" OU "PLUPERFECT" ?

A à Z : 319
322 - 323 - 325

55 ***Choisissez la bonne réponse.***

1. .... any good films lately?
   a. *Did you see* b. *Have you seen* c. *Had you been seeing.*
2. Yesterday, John .... me back the book I .... him.
   a. *gave* ..... *lent* b. *has given* .... *lent* c. *gave* .... *had lent.*
3. Where is Richard? He .... yet.
   a. *did not arrive* b. *hadn't arrived* c. *hasn't arrived.*
4. What was it? Sorry, I .... anything.
   a. *didn't see* b. *haven't seen* c. *hadn't seen*
5. John told me he .... a job in an office.
   a. *has found* b. *had found* c. *found.*
6. They .... in Birmingham since last year.
   a. *have been living* b. *had lived* c. *were living.*
7. Bill said he .... that book before.
   a. *read* b. *was reading* c. *had read.*
8. We .... our dinner when someone knocked at the door.
   a. *have been finishing* b. *have finished* c. *had finished.*
9. I .... in this queue for ages!
   a. *have been standing* b. *was standing* c. *stood.*
10. She .... out of the shop ten minutes ago.
    a. *has come* b. *had come* c. *came.*

L'IMPÉRATIF & "LET"

A à Z
163 - 166 - 186

L'IMPÉRATIF

A à Z : 163

56 ***Regardez attentivement le plan de WELLS, repérez l'endroit où vous êtes, puis répondez aux questions suivantes.***

Ex. : Could you tell me the way to St Cuthbert's Church, please?
→ Certainly. Keep to your right along Princess Road. ***Turn*** *into the second street on the right. The church is on the left.*

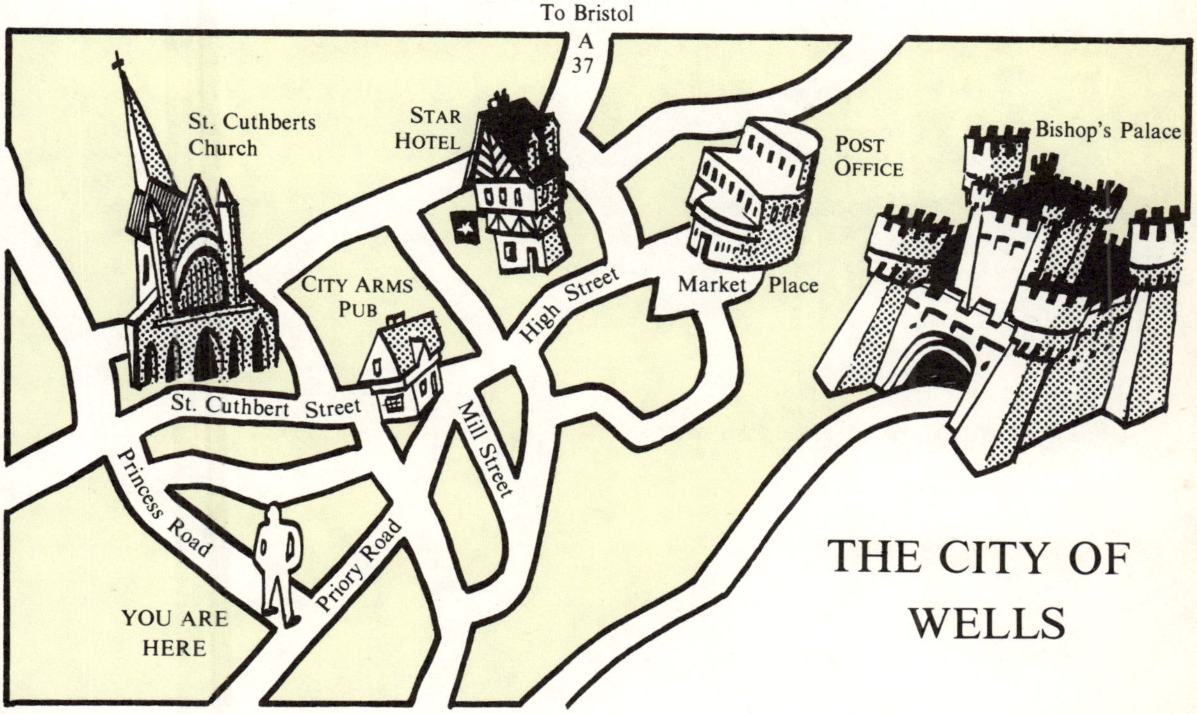

1. Could you tell me the way to the Star Hotel, please?

. . . .

. . . .

. . . .

2. Where is the Post Office, please?

. . . .

. . . .

. . . .

3. I'm looking for the road to Bristol. Could you help me?

. . . .

. . . .

. . . .

4. Could you tell me where Mill Street is, please?

. . . .

. . . .

. . . .

5. Where is the nearest pub, please?

. . . .

. . . .

. . . .

57 ***Donnez des ordres à la forme affirmative ou négative selon le sens.***

Ex. : (Put on) your coat! It's very cold today. – Put on your coat!
(Forget) your keys! The door will be locked. – Don't forget your keys!

1. (Listen) to them! They're laughing at you. ....

....

2. (Wait) for me! I'd like to go with you. ....

....

3. (Show) her that picture! She has never seen it. ....

....

4. (Take) my pen! I need it. ....

....

5. (Switch off) the light! We don't need it any longer. ....

....

6. (Look) at those flowers! They're lovely. ....

....

7. (Tell) him what I said. It's a secret. ....

....

8. (Go away)! I'd like to tell you a story ....

....

"LET"

A à Z : 166 - 186

58 ***Transformez les phrases suivantes.***

Ex. : He wants to see your photos.
*→ **Let him see** your photos.*

1. We want to go to the restaurant.

....

2. She wants to know when you arrive in London.

....

3. I want to finish my exercise.

....

4. They want to watch the football match.

....

5. He wants to use your pen.

....

6. I want to have a look at your paper.

....

7. We want to sing a song.

....

8. She wants to show you her new dress.

....

59 ***Faites des suggestions avec LET'S :***

*Ex. : She'd like to go to the cinema. → **Let's go** to the cinema.*

1. They'd like to have a cup of tea.

....

2. She'd like to stay at home and watch T.V.

....

3. He'd like to play a few records.

....

4. They'd like to buy some sandwiches.

....

5. He'd like to go for a walk.

....

LE FUTUR

"And then he said 'No I won't give you the money'."

A à Z
125 - 126 - 128 - 130 - 132 - 133[1] - 283

WILL & SHALL

A à Z : 126 - 283

60 ***Mettez les verbes entre parenthèses au futur avec WILL ou SHALL, en utilisant les contractions lorsque c'est possible.***

Ex. : They (not arrive) *before Tuesday.*
*→ They **won't arrive** before Tuesday.*

1. Do you think it *(rain)* tomorrow?
   ....
2. It's hot in here. I *(open)* the window?
   ....
3. Mr Morris says he *(be)* back at 9.30.
   ....
4. I'm certain she *(not recognize)* Tom.
   ....
5. I *(have)* my car repaired next week.
   ....
6. When they *(go)* to Birmingham?
   ....
7. We *(have to)* take the bus?
   ....
8. It's too late; Bill *(not catch)* the 8.20 train.
   ....

GOING TO *A à Z : 128*

"My horoscope says you're going to clean the garage, put away the garden hose and clean the gutters today."

61 ***Exprimez une intention avec le futur en "going to" en transformant les phrases suivantes.***

Ex. : His intention is to walk back home.
*→ He **is going to walk** back home.*

1. Their plan is to stay here for a few days.

....

2. My intention is to redecorate my room.

....

3. What does she intend to do?

....

4. Dick's intention is to come back as soon as possible.

....

5. We intend to give you a ring when we arrive in Bath.

....

6. Do you intend to work in Hong-Kong?

....

7. Her plan is tc buy a new stereo.

....

8. I don't intend to take my exam this year.

....

LE FUTUR PROGRESSIF

A à Z : 132

62 ***Mettez les verbes entre parenthèses au futur progressif.***

Ex. : This time next week I (lie) *on a beach.*
*→ This time next week **I'll be lying** on a beach.*

1. You *(need)* your bike tomorrow or can John borrow it?

. . . .

2. We *(wait)* for them when they come out.

. . . .

3. All right, then. I *(see)* you again.

. . . .

4. When we get home, Mother *(stand)* at the door waiting for us.

. . . .

5. It hurts, but don't worry; you *(walk)* again in a few minutes.

. . . .

6. When you next see her, she *(wear)* her new dress.

. . . .

7. He'll call for me at eight but I still *(have)* my breakfast then.

. . . .

8. Dad *(use)* the car tomorrow morning.

. . . .

LE FUTUR ANTÉRIEUR

A à Z : 130

63 ***Transformez les phrases suivantes.***

Ex. : Peter's finishing his homework (by ten).
*→ Peter **will have finished** his homework by ten.*

1. John is leaving *(by the time we arrive).*

. . . .

2. I'm painting the door *(in two hours).*

. . . .

3. She's reading your letter *(when you come back).*

. . . .

4. The Millers are having dinner *(when we call on them).*

. . . .

5. He's cutting the grass *(before tea-time).*

. . . .

6. They're repairing my car *(tomorrow morning).*

. . . .

7. I'm doing my room *(by nine).*

....

8. They're eating everything *(by the time we get to the party).*

....

LE FUTUR ET LES SUBORDONNÉES DE TEMPS

A à Z : 126 - 133[1]

"I'll give her your love when we have our lunch together."

64 ***Mettez le verbe entre parenthèses au présent ou au futur, selon le cas.***

Ex. : I'll give you a ring as soon as I (arrive).
→ *I'll give you a ring as soon as I* ***arrive.***

1. When he *(come)* back, we'll work together.

....

2. I *(go)* on singing until someone tells me to stop.

....

3. As soon as you *(learn)* to drive I'll lend you my car.

....

4. We *(have)* to stay here till the bell rings.

....

5. She'll have a bath before she *(go)* to bed.

....

6. You'll go when I *(tell)* you.

....

7. When I have enough money I *(buy)* that big car.

....

8. John will be very happy when he *(hear)* the good news.

....

A à Z

136 - 167 - 242
à 244

EMPLOI ET FORMATION

*A à Z : 242
243 - 167*

"Well, of course I'm surprised–I'm usually ignored at parties."

65 Mettez les phrases suivantes à la voix passive, sans faire mention de l'agent de l'action.

Ex. : Mary invited Richard to the party.
→ ***Richard was invited to the party.***

1. Paul has just painted the garage door.

   ....

2. They will serve tea in the sitting-room at five.

   ....

3. Someone told me to wait a few minutes.

   ....

4. Mr Smith can't repair my watch.

   ....

5. They should not allow dogs on the beach.

   ....

6. Someone had stolen Bill's car.

   ....

7. They could see some smoke in the distance.

   ....

8. You must read the instructions carefully.

   ....

66 Même exercice, mais avec des phrases dont les verbes sont à la forme progressive.

Ex. : Someone is following you.
→ ***You are being followed.***

1. They are pulling down the old house round the corner.

   ....

2. She was redecorating her room.

   ....

3. Be careful! They are watching you.

   ....

4. They are building a new shopping centre.

   ....

5. The police were still questioning Bob.

   ....

6. Someone is collecting the tickets.

   ....

7. Dick is cleaning the kitchen.

   ....

8. Mary was translating the letter into French.

   ....

67 ***Transformez les phrases suivantes en les mettant à la voix passive et en indiquant l'agent de l'action introduit par BY.***

Ex. : John brought this box.
→ ***This box was brought by John.***

1. A child broke my kitchen window.

....

2. Peter himself built that big house.

....

3. The police are watching them.

....

4. Be careful! That dog could bite you.

....

5. We won't admit children under 13.

....

6. Charles Dickens wrote "David Copperfield".

....

7. His friends are doing the biggest part of the work.

....

8. Ann has seen you walking in the park.

....

LE PASSIF DE "GIVE", "SEND", "SHOW", ETC

68 ***Les phrases suivantes ont deux constructions possibles à la voix passive. Donnez-les (sans mentionner l'agent de l'action).***

Ex. : They gave John a football.
→ ***John was given a football./ A football was given to John.***

1. They showed me a lot of books.

....

....

2. I'll give you a map of London.

....

....

3. Mr Jenkins teaches them Latin.

....

....

4. Peter offered Mary a very nice bunch of flowers.

....

....

5. We have sent a long letter to our parents.

....

....

6. They had promised me a good job.

....

....

7. Richard lent him some money.

....

....

8. He brought me a pen and paper.

....

....

Jeu

WHAT HAVE THEY DONE?

Voici une liste de personnages célèbres :

CHRISTOPHER COLUMBUS - CHARLES DICKENS - ALEXANDER GRAHAM BELL - LEONARDO DA VINCI - WILLIAM SHAKESPEARE - JAMES COOK.

Trouvez ce que chacun a fait et donnez deux réponses à chacune des questions suivantes, une à la voix active, l'autre à la voix passive.

Ex. : Who discovered America?
Christopher Columbus ***discovered*** *America.*
America ***was discovered*** *by Christopher Columbus.*

1. Who wrote *Hamlet?* ....

....

....

2. Who invented the telephone? ....

....

....

3. Who discovered New Zealand? ....

....

....

4. Who painted *Mona Lisa?* ....

....

....

5. Who wrote *David Copperfield?* ....

....

....

LA FORME FRÉQUENTATIVE

A à Z
332 - 339 - 340
348

USED TO. *A à Z : 339 - 332 R³*

69 ***Répondez aux questions suivantes en exprimant une habitude révolue avec USED TO.***

Ex. : Does Mr Smith play football? (younger)
→ ***He used to play football when he was younger***

1. Does Granny ride a bicycle? *(younger).*

. . . .

2. Ann, do you eat many sweets? *(a little girl).*

Ann: I . . . .

3. Do they swim everyday? *(live at the seaside).*

. . . .

4. Does he work a lot in the garden? *(younger).*

. . . .

5. John, do you live in London? *(a child).*

John: I . . . .

6. Does she practise dancing? *(go to school).*

. . . .

7. Do they get up early? *(in those days).*

. . . .

8. Does she wear mini-skirts? *(young).*

. . . .

70 ***Transformez les phrases suivantes en utilisant USED TO.***

Ex. : I no longer play tennis.
→ ***I used to play tennis.***

1. We no longer go to the cinema every week.

. . . .

2. There was a big house round the corner.

. . . .

3. Bill no longer drinks beer.

. . . .

4. Richard no longer works for Shell.

. . . .

5. I collected postcards when I was a child.

. . . .

6. There was a car parked over there.

. . . .

7. Mother told me a story every evening.

. . . .

8. We no longer walk to school.

. . . .

"USED TO" OU "BE USED TO + – ING"?

A à Z : 339 - 340

71 ***Mettez les verbes entre parenthèses à la forme qui convient.***

Ex. : When I was a child, I (eat) *porridge.*
→ *When I was a child I* ***used to eat*** *porridge.*
Don't worry. He (ride) *motorbikes.*
→ *Don't worry. He* ***is used to riding*** *motorbikes.*

1. In those days Mr Jenkins *(smoke)* cigars.

. . . .

2. There *(be)* a bookshop in that street when I was young.

. . . .

3. He is nervous because *(not drive)* sports cars.

. . . .

4. Grandpa *(work)* a lot in the fields when he was younger.

. . . .

5. Don't worry about me. I *(swim)* in the sea.

. . . .

6. In England they *(have)* mutton with mint sauce.

. . . .

7. She *(work)* in London but now she'd rather stay at home.

. . . .

8. We *(live)* in Liverpool in those days.

. . . .

"WOULD" FRÉQUENTATIF

A à Z : 348

72 ***Exprimez une tendance, une habitude ou la répétition d'une action dans le passé à l'aide d'une tournure avec WOULD.***

Ex. : She played the piano (occasionally)
→ *Occasionally she* ***would play*** *the piano.*

1. He sent postcards to his friends *(usually)*.

. . . .

2. They drank a glass of wine *(on Sundays)*.

. . . .

3. My parents watched TV *(every evening)*.

. . . .

4. She went for a walk in the country *(sometimes)*.

. . . .

5. Peter wrote poems *(occasionally).*

....

6. Mother made a big cake *(every week).*

....

7. He had bacon and eggs for his breakfast *(on Saturdays).*

....

8. She gave you a lift *(when you asked her).*

....

Jeu

REMEMBER...

Complétez le dialogue suivant pour aider Grandpa à dire ce qu'il faisait quand il était jeune. Utilisez used to et les indications données entre parenthèses.

Mr Smith: Well, I used to go to school in a small village in Dorset. Where did you go to school?
Grandpa: (Liverpool) ....

....

Mr Smith: And what did you use to do in your free time?
Grandpa: (play football) ....

....

Mr Smith: How interesting! I used to go riding. Did you?
Grandpa: (no, swimming) ....

....

Mr Smith: Really? Well, I used to collect stamps. Did you collect anything?
Grandpa: (yes, postcards) ....

....

Mr Smith: Where did you go for your summer holidays?
Grandpa: (France) ....

....

Mr Smith: We used to go camping in Scotland. Did you use to go camping?
Grandpa: (No) ....

....

Mr Smith: What about the winter? What did you use to do then?
Grandpa: (go skiing) ....

....

....

LE PLURIEL DES NOMS

A à Z

7[3] - 214 - 215 - 216

DÉNOMBRABLES ET INDÉNOMBRABLES *A à Z : 214*

"But of course they're not ants. They're consumers."

73 ***Voici une liste de noms. Répartissez les dans l'une ou l'autre des colonnes ci-dessous.***

milk - table - money - cat - house - water - clock - sugar - tea - bottle - sheep - book - courage - information - idea - man - box

DÉNOMBRABLES	INDÉNOMBRABLES
....	....
....	....
....	....
....	....
....	....
....	....
....	....
....	....
....	....
....	....
....	....

FORMATION DU PLURIEL

A à Z : 214
215 - 216

74 ***Voici une liste de noms au pluriel. Classez-les selon la prononciation de leur finale.***

cups - apples - places - shoes - sandwiches - heads - houses - jobs - lakes - maps - meals - parks - peas - surprises - coats - roads - rooms - offices - planes - pipes.

[s]	[z]	[iz]
....	....	....
....	....	....
....	....	....
....	....	....
....	....	....
....	....	....
....	....	....
....	....	....
....	....	....
....	....	....
....	....	....
....	....	....
....	....	....
....	....	....

75 ***Complétez le tableau suivant :***

SINGULIER	PLURIEL
a baby	....
a leaf	....
....	knives
....	mice
a passer-by	....
....	series
a child	....
a tooth	....
....	potatoes
....	waves
....	families
a brush	....
a sheep	....
....	women
a photo	....

76 ***Complétez les phrases suivantes avec IS ou ARE selon le cas.***

Ex. : There . . . . . people in the front garden.
*→ There **are** people in the front garden.*

1. My luggage . . . . in the back of the car.
2. Bill's hair . . . . black and very long.
3. What colour . . . . his new trousers?
4. Our office furniture . . . . very modern.
5. . . . . there any news about your friend?
6. Peter thinks maths . . . . quite difficult.
7. There has been an accident;
the police . . . . coming.
8. . . . . everybody here?
All right. Let's go.

"Bad news, Joey's dead."

Jeu

CROSSWORDS

Complétez la grille ci-dessous avec le pluriel des noms suivants :

1. a tomato ....
2. a leaf ....
3. a foot ....
4. a country ....
5. a child ....
6. a box ....
7. a gentleman ....
8. a sandwich ....
9. a fish ....
10. a toothbrush ....

ACROSS: 1 - 5 - 6 - 7 - 9 DOWN: 2 - 3 - 4 - 8 - 10

LE GÉNITIF (CAS POSSESSIF)

A à Z
253

LE CAS POSSESSIF *A à Z : 253*

"I hate music–all this was my decorator's idea."

77 ***Complétez les phrases suivantes en employant la forme appropriée du cas possessif sans utiliser de pronoms.***

Ex. : This house belongs to Mr Brown. It's . . . .
→ It's ***Mr Brown's house.***

1. The show lasted two hours. It was a . . . .
2. This handbag belongs to Ann. It's . . . .
3. This school is for girls only. It's . . . .
4. That car belongs to the doctor. It's . . . .
5. Mr and Mrs Green have a dog named Rover. Rover is . . . .
. . . .
6. We took a holiday which lasted a fortnight. It was . . . .
. . . .
7. This shirt belongs to the goal-keeper. It's . . . .
. . . .
8. The Head works in this office. It's . . . .

LE CAS POSSESSIF « INCOMPLET »

A à Z : 253 R.[2]

78 ***Répondez aux questions suivantes.***

Ex. : Whose dog is this? (my neighbour)
→ ***It's my neighbour's.***

1. Whose coat is this? *(Mr Jenkins)* . . . .
2. Whose book is this? *(my sister)* . . . .
3. Are these your pens? *(Bill)* No, ...
4. Whose car is this? *(my parents)* . . . .
5. Is this Mr Smith's garden? *(Mr Brown)* No, ...
6. Whose house is this? *(Mr and Mrs Smith)* . . . .
7. Whose bags are these? *(the children)* . . . .
8. Is this your hat? *(Henry)* No, ...

LE « DOUBLE POSSESSIF »

A à Z : 253 R.[3]

79 ***Transformez les phrases suivantes.***

Ex. : Mrs Brown is one of my mother's friends.
→ Mrs Brown is ***a friend of my mother's.***

1. Patricia is one of Jenny's sisters.
. . . .
2. Bill is wearing one of his brother's sweaters.
. . . .

3. This is probably one of John's ideas.

. . . .

4. I've borrowed one of my father's ties.

. . . .

5. Isn't it one of Mary's photos?

. . . .

6. This is one of my neighbour's cats.

. . . .

7. I think it is one of your books.

. . . .

8. Peter Jenkins is one of Richard's uncles.

. . . .

LA TRADUCTION DE « CHEZ » *A à Z : 253 R.²*

80 ***Répondez aux questions suivantes en vous servant de la liste ci-dessous.***

baker - butcher - grocer - hairdresser - dentist - doctor - greengrocer - florist - chemist

Ex. : Where did you get these flowers?
→ ***I got them at the florist's.***

1. Where do you go when you don't feel well?

....

2. Where did you get this very good meat?

....

3. This bread is very good. Where did you buy it?

....

4. I'd like to buy some vegetables. Where should I go?

....

5. Where do you go when you want to have your teeth examined?

....

6. I had my hair cut. Where did I go?

....

7. Where can we buy food?

....

8. Where do you go when you need some medicine?

....

L'ADJECTIF

A à Z
7 - 8 - 28 - 66 à 70 - 218 - 251 - 345 - 346

LES ADJECTIFS QUALIFICATIFS

A à Z : 7 - 8 - 28 - 66 - 70

"That's odd, it's an imitation one."

81 ***Les éléments des phrases suivantes ont été mélangés. Remettez-les en bon ordre.***

Ex. : bought/light blue/John/tie/a.
→ ***John bought a light blue tie.***

1. parents/village/live/small/my/a/in.

....

2. trees/are/tall/along/there/streets/the.

....

3. cottage/I/round/corner/like/old/the/the.

....

4. lovely/there/park/is/river/along/a/the.

....

5. walks/in/there/evening/the/pleasant/to have/it is.

....

6. very old/the/stands/a/hill/of/on top/church.

....

7. the/building/near/white/Market Place/is/school/the.

....

8. happy/my/say/are/parents/they.

....

82 ***Faites des phrases du type A > B (comparatif de supériorité).***

Ex. : English is (> easy) Chinese.
→ ***English is easier than Chinese.***

1. I think the book is (> *interesting)* film.

....

2. Their house is (> *big)* mine.

....

3. Peter has always been (> *good at maths)* anyone.

....

4. He said that cats were (> *intelligent)* dogs.

....

5. The weather can't be (> *bad)* it is today!

....

6. Mr Simpson is much (> *old)* his wife.

....

7. Her dress is (> *expensive)* Ann's.

....

8. He has always told us that health was (> *important)* money.

....

83 ***Faites des phrases du type A > B (comparatif de supériorité), A ≠ B (comparatif d'inégalité), A = B (comparatif d'égalité), ou A < (comparatif d'infériorité)***

Ex. : She said that girls were (= clever*) boys.*
→ She said that girls were ***as clever as*** *boys.*

1. Peter says that Geography is (> *hard)* history.

....

2. Our car is *(< comfortable)* Mr Brown's.

....

3. I think that things are (≠ *good)* they used to be.

....

4. That bus is (= *late)* usual!

....

5. Is it true that girls are (> *sensitive)* boys?

....

6. Your suitcase is (≠ *heavy)* I thought it was.

....

7. This food is (< *good)* I expected.

....

8. I think that John is (= *clever)* his brother.

....

"Mirror, mirror on the wall – who is the fairest one of all?"

84 *Mettez les adjectifs entre parenthèses au superlatif de supériorité.*

Ex. : This is (interesting) *film I've ever seen.*
→ *This is* ***the most interesting*** *film I've ever seen.*

1. The school is *(big)* building in the street.
....
2. The *(tall)* boy in our school is a basketball player.
....
3. Oxford is *(old)* university in Britain.
....
4. She thinks that *(elegant)* dresses are Dior's.
....
5. For him, being in good health is *(important)* thing.
....
6. And now, here is *(late)* news.
....
7. I think Ann is *(pretty)* girl in town.
....
8. That is probably *(good)* book I have ever read.
....

85 *Transformez les phrases suivantes.*

Ex. : He's walking faster every minute.
→ *He's walking* ***faster and faster.***

1. Your English is getting better every day.
....
2. I think my job is getting more interesting.
....
3. Cars are getting more comfortable these days.
....
4. Don't you think we are going slower?
....
5. For him, money is getting more important.
....
6. He's getting up earlier every morning.
....
7. Our house is getting older.
....
8. She opened her eyes wider every minute.
....

"I've just noticed. You're left-footed."

86 ***Formez des adjectifs composés comme dans l'exemple ci-dessous.***

Ex. : She's a girl with blue eyes.
*→ She's a **blue-eyed** girl.*

1. Mr Brown is a man with broad shoulders.

....

2. John always uses his left hand.

....

3. She is very tolerant. She's a girl with a broad mind.

....

4. Richard is a boy with dark hair.

....

5. Peter is a man with only one arm.

....

6. She wears glasses because she's a woman with short sight.

....

7. He was very sad. He was a man with a broken heart.

....

8. They are people with a good nature.

....

LES ADJECTIFS INTERROGATIFS

A à Z : 345 - 346

87 ***Complétez les phrases suivantes avec WHICH ou WHAT.***

*Ex. : . . . . . is it made of? → **What** is it made of?*
. . . . . way shall we go, up or down the street?
*→ **Which** way shall we go ... ?*

1. .... one will you have – the big one or the small one?
2. .... sort of films do you like seeing?
3. .... was the weather like in Britain last week?
4. .... did you do that for?
5. .... is better – peas or carrots?
6. .... is the matter with her?
7. .... of the two boys do you like better?
8. .... stupid game is he playing now?

88 ***Posez des questions qui correspondent aux réponses suivantes.***

Ex. : I prefer the blue one.
*→ **Which** one do you prefer?*

1. It's Mary Norton's umbrella.

   ....

2. I'm looking at that very nice car over there.

   ....

3. She likes Richard better.

   ....

4. We listened to a programme about the Beatles on the radio.

   ....

5. He's interested in pop music.

   ....

6. She's tall and thin; she's got long fair hair and blue eyes.

   ....

7. I'll take the little red one.

   ....

8. It's made of plastic.

   ....

LES ADJECTIFS POSSESSIFS *A à Z : 251*

89 ***Complétez les phrases suivantes à l'aide de l'adjectif possessif qui convient.***

Ex. : Mrs Smith was accompanied by . . . . . husband.
→ Mrs Smith was accompanied by ***her*** *husband.*

1. Excuse me, Tom. Can I borrow . . . . pen?
2. Bob and . . . . sister have just sent a letter to . . . . mother.
3. Yes, that car is nice, but I don't like . . . . colour.
4. Look! Mary's just had . . . . hair cut.
5. Hey! Don't take . . . . book. I need it.
6. Mr Jenkins has bought . . . . wife some flowers.
7. My neighbours would like to sell . . . . house.
8. A man was standing there, with . . . . hands in . . . . pockets.

LES ADJECTIFS NUMÉRAUX *A à Z : 218*

90 ***Traduisez les groupes de mots suivants. Les nombres doivent apparaître en toutes lettres.***

Ex. : 1.450 one thousand, four hundred and fifty
7,25 seven point twenty five.

- 13 : . . . .
- 689 : . . . .
- 3.523 : . . . .
- 3/5 : . . . .
- 9,81 : . . . .
- 4.790 : . . . .
- 10.202 : . . . .
- 3,14 : . . . .
- 1/100,000 : . . . .

91 ***Écrivez les opérations suivantes en toutes lettres.***

Ex. : 12 – 5 = 7 : twelve minus five equals seven

1. 9 + 6 = 15 . . . .
2. 5 x 12 = 60 . . . .
3. 24 : 3 = 8 . . . .
4. 43 – 21 = 22 . . . .

Jeu

LET'S COMPARE

1. *Lisez attentivement ce petit paragraphe :*

John, Richard and David work in a bank. John is thin, and Richard is thinner than John. But even Richard isn't as thin as David. David is the thinnest man in the bank.

Maintenant, complétez les silhouettes de John, Richard et David.

2. *Faites de courts paragraphes comme au n° 1 :*

– Rome, London and Paris are in Europe. They're big cities.

– A Rolls Royce, a Triumph and a Mini are English cars. They're comfortable.

LES PRONOMS

A à Z
229 - 252 - 261
à 262 - 345

LES PRONOMS PERSONNELS *A à Z : 261*

"... and we know that you know that we know that you know that we know you're in there."

92 ***Remplacez le nom en italique par un pronom personnel, et effectuez toutes les transformations nécessaires. Attention aux prépositions TO et FOR.***

*Ex. : Give Bill a present. → Give **it** to Bill.*
*Give Bill a present. → Give **it** to **him.***

1. Tell *Patricia* to come here immediately.

....

2. Send *Mr and Mrs Watson a postcard.*

....

3. Show Richard *the newspaper.*

....

4. Pass *your sister the salt.*

....

5. Bring me *your exercise-book.*

....

6. Lend *John* some money.

....

7. Get Mother *the TV magazine.*

....

8. Tell *your parents* the truth.

....

93 ***Complétez le texte suivant à l'aide des pronoms personnels qui conviennent.***

Suddenly Helen started because .... had heard a noise in the passage; then .... stopped and .... knew that there was someone outside the door, listening. .... stared at .... in a panic. Then .... sat on the floor and did not move at all. The man by her side did not move either because .... was dead.

LES PRONOMS RÉFLÉCHIS

A à Z : 262

94 ***Répondez aux questions en vous servant de pronoms réfléchis.***

Ex. : Did someone wash your car for you?
*→ **No, I washed it myself.***

1. Did your mother make your bed for you?
– No, I ....
2. The children had a picnic. Did their parents organize it?
– No, the children ....
3. Did you teach Jenny to play the piano?
– No, she ....
4. Will you buy this magazine for me?
– No, buy ....
5. Did you have this house built? ....
– No, we ....

6. Does his wife write his letters for him?
– No, he ....
7. Did you open that door?
– No, it ....
8. Did you have a good time?
– Yes, we enjoyed ....

LES PRONOMS POSSESSIFS *A à Z : 252*

"You have a go in ours, and we'll have a go in yours, okay?"

95 ***Transformez les phrases suivantes avec des pronoms possessifs.***

Ex. : This is her business, not your business.
→ This is her business, not ***yours.***

1. Bill's car isn't as fast as my car.

....

2. I know Mr Brown very well. He is one of my friends.

....

3. I've lost my pen. Can I borrow your pen?

....

4. This is not your umbrella; it's her umbrella.

....

5. I think Derek is one of his cousins.

....

6. We were invited by one of our uncles.

....

7. This is our house; it is bigger than their house.

....

8. My job is more interesting than your job.

....

LES PRONOMS INTERROGATIFS

A à Z : 345

96 ***Complétez les phrases suivantes à l'aide de WHO (pronom), de WHAT ou de WHICH (adjectifs ou pronoms).***

Ex. : . . . . . is that boy in the red jumper?
*→ **Who** is that boy . . . . .?*

1. . . . . is your telephone number?
2. . . . . of these books do you like best?
3. . . . . did you give my pen to?
4. . . . . is this cake made of?
5. . . . . do you want to be when you grow up?
– A teacher.
6. Tell me . . . . seats you would like.
7. Let me know . . . . train you'll be arriving on.
8. Do you know . . . . all these people are?

"What kind of a Hippopot-Am-I."

LE PRONOM "ONE" COMME SUBSTITUT DU NOM

A à Z : 229

97 ***Évitez les répétitions en utilisant ONE ou ONES (substitut du nom) dans les phrases suivantes.***

Ex. : Will she buy a blue dress or a white dress?
*→ Will she buy a blue dress or a white **one**?*

1. Which book do you want? – The red book.
. . . .
2. I haven't a pen. Can you lend me a pen?
. . . .
3. These small apples are good but I prefer big red apples.
. . . .
4. They've just bought a house. It's a big house.
. . . .
5. It's in that drawer – the drawer with a key in the lock.
. . . .
6. They think our ideas are good ideas.
. . . .
7. My cheap camera seems to be just as good as Bill's expensive camera.
. . . .
8. There is a right answer and a wrong answer.
. . . .

LES ARTICLES

A à Z

1 - 2 - 329 à 331

L'ARTICLE INDÉFINI "A/AN"

A à Z : 1, 2, 330 - 331

"The TV film of your operation was such a success that the producer wants you to do a series."

98 ***Complétez les phrases suivantes avec A, AN ou Ø.***

Ex. : Peter's .... friend of mine.
*→ Peter's **a** friend of mine.*

1. I've just read .... book about .... English cars.
2. John goes to .... school now and he wears .... uniform.
3. It took me .... hour to do this exercise!
4. .... English people are said to like .... tea very much.
5. What .... big sandwich she's eating!
6. .... life is not so easy as it used to be.
7. Richard is .... doctor and his wife .... English teacher.
8. She dresses in .... perfect taste.

L'ARTICLE DÉFINI "THE" *A à Z : 330 - 331*

99 ***Complétez les phrases suivantes avec THE ou Ø.***

Ex. : Do you like . . . . . tea? – Yes, I do, and I love . . . . . tea you make.
*→ Do you like Ø tea? – Yes, and I love **the** tea you make.*

1. Where is . . . . . book I put on . . . . . table?
2. . . . . . French are said to be . . . . . good cooks.
3. . . . . . last time I saw him, he said he was going to . . . . . U.S.A.
4. He never watches . . . . . T.V. and never listens to . . . . . radio.
5. . . . . . baseball isn't a popular game in . . . . . Europe.
6. She likes . . . . . music and she plays . . . . . piano very well.
7. . . . . . Queen Elizabeth II had a holiday in . . . . . Alps . . . . . last year.
8. . . . . . English teacher is . . . . . kindest man I know!

"A/AN", "THE" ou Ø? *A à Z : 1 - 2 329 - 330 - 331*

100 ***Complétez les paragraphes suivants.***

1. . . . . post is one of . . . . most useful public services; it plays . . . . important part in life of . . . . society, both in . . . . town and in . . . . country. In . . . . farms which are . . . . long way from . . . . village, ... postman is . . . . welcome visitor who brings . . . . news from . . . . rest of . . . . world.
2. One of . . . . most interesting monuments we visited was . . . . Tower of London. Not very far from . . . . City, close to . . . . banks of . . . . river Thames stands . . . . old building which was by turns . . . . fortress, ... palace and . . . . prison.
3. One morning, not long ago, I went out for . . . . walk. It was . . . . warm, sunny morning. No wind, just . . . . few very white clouds like . . . . marks on . . . . blue sky. In . . . . distance I could see . . . . lovely pink cottage.

LES INDÉFINIS DE QUANTITÉ

A à Z

17 - 94 - 119 - 108 - 206 - 219 - 236 - 293 à 295

SOME, ANY, NO, NOT ANY

A à Z : 293 294 - 219

101 ***Complétez les phrases suivantes avec SOME ou ANY.***

Ex. : I'd like . . . . water, please.
*→ I'd like **some** water, please.*

1. Have you . . . . sugar? We need . . . . for our cake.
2. The Johnsons haven't . . . . children.
3. Mr Black has . . . . flowers in his garden.
4. We have hardly . . . . tea left!
5. He gave you . . . . wine, didn't he?
6. Are there . . . . stamps in that drawer? Yes, there are . . . .
7. I can see . . . . people walking down the street.
8. You'll need . . . . money if you're going shopping.

102 ***Dans les phrases suivantes, remplacez NOT ANY par NO.***

Ex. : There isn't any milk in the fridge.
*→ There is **no** milk in the fridge.*

1. There weren't any stamps in the machine.

. . . .

2. He hasn't got any friends in London.

. . . .

3. I see you haven't any pen. Take mine.

. . . .

4. Jim can't open the door. He hasn't got any key.

. . . .

5. There aren't any plates in that cupboard.

. . . .

6. We haven't got any ice-cream.

. . . .

7. There aren't any letters for me.

. . . .

8. Sorry. There aren't any seats left for that concert.

. . . .

LES COMPOSÉS DE "SOME", "ANY", "NO" *A à Z : 295*

103 ***Complétez les phrases suivantes par des composés de SOME, ANY ou NO formés avec THING, BODY ou WHERE.***

Ex. : Where's my pen? I can't find it . . . . .
*→ I can't find it **anywhere.***

"Do you think there's somewhere up there where they don't play football?"

1. He's very busy. He can't see . . . . today.
2. You look hungry. We'll give you . . . . to eat.
3. Where have they been? – They haven't been . . . .
4. I rang the doorbell but apparently there was . . . . in.
5. Show it again, please. I couldn't see . . . .
6. Where's my key? It must be . . . . in this room.
7. They all said . . . . except me. I had . . . . to say.
8. . . . . has locked the door. . . . . can go out!

"MUCH" OU "MANY"? *A à Z : 206*

104 ***Complétez les phrases suivantes avec MUCH ou MANY selon le cas.***

Ex. : Little Jane eats . . . . . sweets.
*→ Little Jane eats **many** sweets.*

1. There is not . . . . work to be done.
2. How . . . . chairs are there in that room?
3. She never eats . . . . at breakfast.
4. . . . . people go shopping on Saturdays.
5. Will it take . . . . time to do this job?
6. I haven't got . . . . money; I can't buy . . . . books.
7. He made ten spelling mistakes in as . . . . lines!
8. How . . . . milk do you want?

"I'm afraid my wife doesn't trust me much."

LITTLE, A LITTLE, FEW, A FEW *A à Z : 119*

105 ***Remplacez les expressions en italique par LITTLE, A LITTLE, FEW, ou A FEW.***

Ex. : Hardly any *people came to the concert.*
→ ***Few*** *people came to the concert.*

1. Would you like *some* more tea?

. . . .

2. Let's talk about *several* things before we go.

. . . .

3. There is *not much* we can do to help them.

. . . .

4. We'll probably spend *two or three* days at the seaside.

. . . .

5. *Not many* people can swim across the Channel.

. . . .

6. Patricia understands *a small quantity of* German.

. . . .

7. I am not an expert, but I know *something* about birds.

. . . .

8. We have only *a small piece of* bread left.

. . . .

"ALL", "EACH", "EVERY" ET SES COMPOSÉS *A à Z : 17 - 94*

106 ***Choisissez la bonne réponse.***

1. He visits his grandmother . . . . week.
   a. *every* b. *each* c. *all.*
2. The sun shone . . . . time in New York.
   a. *all* b. *every* c. *all the.*
3. We had brought . . . . our food with us.
   a. *each* b. *all* c. *every.*
4. . . . . knew that it would rain very soon.
   a. *Everybody* b. *Everything* c. *Each.*
5. This shop sells . . . . needed for camping.
   a. *everyone* b. *everything* c. *everybody.*
6. There are buses to the town centre . . . . . . ten minutes.
   a. *each* b. *all* c. *every.*

7. Look! He has an apple in . . . . hand.

a. *every* b. *each* c. *everyone.*

8. I couldn't find my key though I looked .... for it.
   a. *everything* b. *everywhere* c. *everyone.*
9. .... the pupils brought their dinners in baskets.
   a. *each* b. *all* c. *every of.*
10. We had to drive 15 miles .... way to take him to the station.
   a. *every* b. *all* c. *each.*

ENOUGH *A à Z : 108 - 236*

107 ***Placez ENOUGH au bon endroit dans les phrases suivantes.***

Ex. : You know well ***enough*** *that I haven't* ***enough*** *time.*

1. They haven't food to feed everyone.
   ....
   ....
2. Is it hot for him to go swimming?
   ....
   ....
3. She's pretty, I suppose, but I don't admire her.
   ....
   ....
4. Have you money to pay for the book?
   ....
   ....
5. He's had to eat.
   ....
   ....
6. Stupidly, I lost my umbrella.
   ....
   ....

"The two gentlemen were kind enough to give me a lift."

7. John ran quickly to pass the speed test.
   ....
   ....
8. This book is easy for a six-year-old child to read.
   ....

LE DIALOGUE

A à Z

88 - 223 - 292 - 303 à 307

RÉPONSES COURTES

A à Z : 88
306[1] - 223

108 ***Donnez des réponses courtes aux questions suivantes, comme dans l'exemple ci-dessous.***

Ex. : Has Richard finished his work? No ...
→ ***No, he hasn't.***

1. Can you read these small letters? Of course I ....
2. Will they be there at ten o'clock? No, ...
3. Do you think they'll understand? Yes, I ....
4. Have you ever been to the U.S.A.? No, we ....
5. Did you see that film on T.V.? Yes, we ....
6. Are they going to leave early in the morning? No, ...
7. Would she lend us money if we asked her? No, ...
8. Had John come here before? Of course ....

109 ***Donnez des réponses courtes aux questions suivantes (avec reprise d'un auxiliaire ou d'un modal).***

Ex. : Who will go shopping? Peter.
→ ***Peter will.***

1. Who can read German? Patricia ....
2. Who will wash the dishes? I ....
3. Who's got a piece of paper? Richard ....
4. Who knocked at the door? Mrs Smith ....
5. Who had sent that letter? Jennifer ....
6. Who came here by bus? John ....
7. Who would accept to go? Robert ....
8. Who saw what happened? My brother ....

QUESTION TAGS

A à Z : 303 - 304

110 ***Complétez les phrases suivantes avec des "question tags".***

Ex. : You'd been there before, ... → ***hadn't you?***

1. They weren't waiting for us, ...
2. John can speak Italian, ...
3. The Lawsons arrived yesterday, ...
4. Richard likes playing the piano, ...
5. Let's have a cup of tea, ...
6. She can swim, ...
7. Peter was very pleased, ...
8. You didn't call me, ...
9. I am too early, ...
10. It's very difficult, ...
11. She came here three days ago, ...
12. You've already been to the U.S.A., ...
13. They wouldn't like me to go away, ...
14. We needn't give you more details, ...
15. You shouldn't drive so fast, ...
16. He can't do it now, ...
17. Bill takes the bus every morning, ...
18. You aren't sleeping, ...
19. They will give us a ring, ...
20. We don't have to go there, ...
21. It doesn't really hurt, ...
22. You couldn't see John, ...
23. She had to answer immediately, ...
24. They won't send us a letter, ...

« MOI AUSSI / MOI NON PLUS »

A à Z : 307 - 99

111 ***Exprimez la « conformité positive » grâce à SO + AUXILIAIRE (ou MODAL) + SUJET après chacune des phrases suivantes.***

Ex. : They went to London yesterday. (we)
→ ***So did we.***

1. Peter's very good at History. *(his brother).*

. . . .

2. He's understood everything. *(I)*

. . . .

3. I know Bill Grant very well. *(Patricia)*

. . . .

4. The Richardsons will be there by 10. *(you)*

. . . .

5. I'd be very pleased to meet them. *(they)*

. . . .

6. Your brother can run very fast. *I*

. . . .

7. You were very late to school. *(she)*

. . . .

8. He'd seen them before. *(we)*

. . . .

112 ***Exprimez la « conformité négative » en utilisant EITHER, puis NEITHER.***

Ex. : They haven't heard of him. (we)
→ ***We haven't either / Neither have we.***

1. Your friends shouldn't stay here. *(you)*

. . . .

2. I couldn't see anything! *(we)*

. . . .

3. He won't go to work tomorrow. *(she)*

. . . .

4. Bill isn't very good at maths. *(I)*

. . . .

5. I wouldn't like to work with them. *(we)*

. . . .

6. She doesn't want to leave now. *(you)*

. . . .

7. John hadn't seen that car before. *(she)*

. . . .

8. I don't know where my keys are. *(I)*

. . . .

REPRISE AVEC "SO" *A à Z : 292*

113 ***Transformez les réponses suivantes en remplaçant une proposition entière par SO.***

Ex. : Is Peter at school? → Well, I think he is at school.
*→ **Well, I think so.***

1. Will they accept to do the job? – I don't think they will accept to do it.

....

2. Did they hear what we said? – Well, I'm afraid they heard it.

....

3. Does John like pop music? – We imagine he likes it.

....

4. Did she enjoy herself? – I hope she enjoyed herself.

....

5. Will you be going to the football match? – I don't suppose we'll be going.

....

6. Can he play cricket? – I think he can play cricket.

....

7. Will she need help? – No, I don't expect she'll need help.

....

8. Will they be ready tomorrow? – Yes, I believe they'll be ready.

....

LA SUBORDINATION

A à Z

93 - 103 - 111 - 120 - 133 - 158 - 258² - 263 à 265

PRONOMS & ADVERBES RELATIFS

A à Z : 263 - 264 265 - 111

114 ***Complétez les phrases suivantes avec WHO ou WHICH***

Ex. : Joe is the boy .... is wearing a blue jumper.
*→ Joe is the boy **who** is wearing a blue jumper.*

1. Take the exercise book .... is lying on that table.
2. Their house for .... they paid a fortune is now in ruins.
3. There was a man .... called to see you while you were out.
4. She said I was late, ... wasn't true.
5. This is the girl .... was in the library yesterday.
6. There's someone .... is waiting for you at the door.
7. Peter, ... bought a car yesterday, has just had an accident.
8. Can you read the name .... is written on that box?

115 ***Transformez les phrases suivantes comme dans l'exemple ci-dessous.***

Ex. : This is the boy about whom we were speaking.
→ ***This is the boy we were speaking about.***

1. Here is the key for which you were looking.

....

2. I took all the photos at which you are looking.

....

3. The book to which I wanted to refer was not in the library.

....

4. I like the music to which you are listening.

....

5. This is the kind of story in which I am interested.

....

6. I think you know the people with whom I stayed.

....

7. This is the man to whom I gave it.

....

8. The chair on which you are sitting is an antique.

....

"I am he through whom enquiry may be made."

116 ***Choisissez la bonne réponse.***

1. He didn't believe .... I said.
   a. *that* b. *what* c. *which.*
2. She did .... she could, ... wasn't much.
   a. *which – what* b. *that – that* c. *what – which.*
3. John was the only person .... saw the difficulty.
   a. *who* b. *which* c. *whom.*
4. Show me .... you've got in your bag.
   a. *that* b. *who* c. *what.*
5. I'm sorry, I don't know .... to do.
   a. *which* b. *who* c. *what.*
6. If only you'd told me .... they were!
   a. *that* b. *who* c. *whom.*
7. They want to finish the job in two days, ... is impossible.
   a. *what* b. *that* c. *which.*
8. Thank you for .... you have done.
   a. *which* b. *what* c. *whom.*
9. He's upset because he didn't see .... he wanted.
   a. *what* b. *that* c. *which.*
10. She is always the last .... goes.
    a. *whom* b. *what* c. *who.*

117 ***Complétez les phrases suivantes avec un des mots suivants : WHATEVER, WHICHEVER, WHOEVER, WHEREVER, WHENEVER, HOWEVER.***

Ex. : Do ..... you like.
→ Do ***whatever*** *you like.*

1. This picture looks wrong, ... you look at it.
2. There's no reservation. You can sit .... you like.
3. I'll take .... books you don't want.
4. We'll be at home all day. You can come .... you want.
5. .... gets the job will have a lot of work to do.
6. They have to go on, ... difficulties they meet.
7. We're going, ... happens.
8. .... rings, tell him I'm out.
9. She comes from Bolimba, ... that may be.
10. I couldn't do it, ... hard I tried.

CONJONCTIONS

A à Z : 93 - 103
120 - 133 - 158

"I miss the good old days when all we had to worry about was nouns and verbs."

118 ***Choisissez la bonne réponse :***

1. .... it was raining, she went out without an umbrella.
   a. *In case,* b. *Since* c. *Although.*
2. We won't meet again .... I've left.
   a. *after* b. *as long as* c. *since.*
3. What were you doing .... I was working in the garden?
   a. *while* b. *as* c. *after.*
4. What did she do .... she met him?
   a. *while* b. *since* c. *before.*
5. Give us a ring .... you get there.
   a. *since* b. *as soon as* c. *as far as.*
6. He will help you .... he can.
   a. *as much as* b. *so that* c. *though.*
7. Where have they been .... I last saw them?
   a. *when* b. *as soon as* c. *since.*
8. Don't come .... I telephone.
   a. *since* b. *as* c. *unless.*
9. Let's wait here .... the rain stops.
   a. *till* b. *because* c. *since.*
10. .... it is necessary, I can come at seven.
   a. *If* b. *Though* c. *Until.*

119 ***Transformez les phrases suivantes en commençant par le mot indiqué et en utilisant la conjonction entre parenthèses.***

Ex. : Drink that and you'll be sick! (if)
If . . . . .
→ ***If you drink that you'll be sick!***

1. He spoke slowly and we could understand him. *(so that)*
He . . . .
. . . .
2. They asked me to do it and I did it *(because)*
I . . . .
. . . .
3. Work harder or you will fail. *(unless)*
You . . . .
. . . .
4. We were out and it began to rain *(while)*
It . . . .
. . . .

"Do you mind if I smoke?"

5. The weather was very bad, but the plane took off. *(though)*
The plane . . . .
6. It takes me all the morning but I'll do it. *(even if)*
I . . . .
7. Promise to help her and she will go away. *(until)*
She won't . . . .
8. I did my best for them and they were angry! *(even though)*
They . . . .

120 ***Transformez les phrases suivantes en employant une tournure avec IF. Attention à l'emploi des temps.***

Ex. : he didn't see the red light, so he didn't stop.
→ ***If he had seen the red light, he would have stopped.***

1. I didn't know where she lived, so I didn't visit her.
. . . .
2. They took the train because their car was being repaired.
. . . .
3. We didn't go for a walk because it was raining.
. . . .
4. He didn't sing clearly, so we didn't recognize the song.
. . . .
5. I missed my bus, so I was late.
. . . .
6. She didn't speak French, so she didn't get the job.
. . . .
7. You didn't look ill, so I didn't send for a doctor.
. . . .

8. He didn't ask her, so she didn't tell him the story.

. . . .

121 ***Mettez chaque verbe entre parenthèses au temps qui convient.***

Ex. : We'll start as soon as they (be) ready.
→ We'll start as soon as they ***are*** *ready.*

1. He'll give her this message when he *(meet)* her.

. . . .

. . . .

2. You'll have a biscuit as soon as we *(get)* home.

. . . .

. . . .

3. As long as he *(be)* here I'll have more work to do.

. . . .

. . . .

4. They said they would give us a ring as soon as they *(reach)* Hong Kong.

. . . .

. . . .

5. She'll study music while she *(be)* in London.

. . . .

. . . .

6. They won't be happy till you *(promise)* to go with them.

. . . .

. . . .

7. I'm sure he'll raise his hat when he *(see)* her.

. . . .

. . . .

8. Until I *(get)* a letter from him, I won't know.

. . . .

. . . .

"I won't be sorry when somebody gets this perspective problem sorted out."

L'INTERROGATION & L'EXCLAMATION

A à Z

84 - 112 - 113 - 154 à 157 - 290

L'INTERROGATION

A à Z : 84 - 154 à 157
258[1] - 271

"How are things otherwise?"

122 ***Posez des questions commençant par HOW correspondant aux affirmations suivantes.***

Ex. : Richard is fifteen years old.
→ ***How old is Richard?***

1. We go to London every week.

. . . .

2. The Carters have been living here for ten years.

. . . .

3. The post office is about a half mile from here.

. . . .

4. The Eiffel Tower is more than 300 metres high.

. . . .

5. Patricia has been studying Italian since 1986.

. . . .

6. Paul is six foot two!

. . . .

7. There are 600 pupils in my school.

. . . .

8. I've been waiting for ten minutes.

. . . .

123 ***Posez des questions correspondant aux réponses suivantes.***

Ex. : He was playing with John.
→ ***Who was he playing with?***

1. This box is made of wood.

. . . .

2. It depends on the weather being fine.

. . . .

3. He's looking at Sheila.

. . . .

4. They're interested in old books.

. . . .

5. Bob is talking to Robert.

. . . .

6. These people come from Bristol.

. . . .

7. We're listening to an opera on the radio.

. . . .

8. She's waiting for the next train.

. . . .

124 ***Rapportez les questions suivantes (voir A à Z : 84).***

Ex. : "Where is John?" Paul asked.
*→ **Paul asked where John was.***

1. "Who is going to help me?" Mr Jenkins asked us.

....

2. "When is the next bus?" Bill asked me.

....

3. "How long have you been waiting?" they asked him.

....

4. "Can I speak to Patricia?" John asked.

....

5. "What's the matter with her?" he asked.

....

6. "Which one do you prefer?" Bob will ask me.

....

7. "How much does it cost?" she asked.

....

8. "Where do you think they will go?" Mrs Benson asked me.

....

L'EXCLAMATION

A à Z : 112
113 - 290

125 ***Faites des phrases exclamatives commençant par HOW ou par WHAT selon le cas.***

Ex. : This is a lovely *place.* → ***How lovely this place is!***
This is a lovely place. → ***What a lovely place** (this is)!*

1. Their house was *dirty* ....
2. You look *well* ....
3. This is a good *idea* ....
4. They showed great *courage* ....
5. Richard is a *fool* ....
6. This is a silly *book* ....
7. It was an *important* decision ....
8. The garden was *beautiful* ....
9. You were very *kind* ....
10. He is a very fast *driver* ....

126 ***Transformez les phrases suivantes comme dans l'exemple ci-dessous.***

Ex. : It's lovely. → ***Isn't it lovely!***

1. They look strange ....
2. It was very surprising ....
3. That noise is awful ....
4. It's difficult ....
5. They're very busy ....
6. She was careful ....
7. It's a very common flower ....
8. That film was dull ....

127 ***Faites des phrases exclamatives avec SO ou SUCH selon le cas.***

Ex. : It's lovely *around here.* → ***It's so lovely around here!***
It's a beautiful day. → ***It's such a beautiful day!***

1. The news gave me *a shock.*

....

2. They have been *good friends* to me.

....

3. My neighbours are *nice.*

....

4. It's *a big cake.*

....

5. I think Bob is *clever.*

....

6. We've had *a good time.*

....

7. I had never seen *a lovely garden.*

....

8. She's *a good pianist.*

....

L'INFINITIF & LA FORME EN "-ING"

A à Z
165 à 170 - 122 - 187^2 - 174 à 176

L'INFINITIF

A à Z : 165 - 166 - 167^1 168 - 170 - 122 - 187^2

128 ***Faites précéder les infinitifs entre parenthèses par TO lorsqu'il le faut.***

Ex. : He wants (go) *now. All right. He can* (go).
→ *He wants* **to go** *now. All right he can* **go.**

1. He made me *(do)* my exercise all over again.

....

2. Could you *(tell)* me where the station is, please?

....

3. Please let us *(know)* when you arrive.

....

4. Would you ike *(come)* with us?

....

5. I'd better *(leave)* early tomorrow morning.

....

6. We saw them *(throw)* stones and *(run)* away.

....

7. It's difficult for them *(understand)* what you say.

....

8. His father wants him *(be)* an engineer.

....

129 ***Remplacez les expressions soulignées par des infinitifs ou des constructions avec un infinitif.***

Ex. : She was the first girl who finished *the race.*
→ *She was the first girl* ***to finish*** *the race.*

1. I was surprised *when I heard* that they had moved.

....

2. It's important *that the children should arrive* in time.

....

3. Have you got a key *with which we could open* that door?

....

4. We were late and there was no place *where to sit.*

....

5. He was the last boy *who left* the house.

....

6. Armstrong was the first man *who walked* on the moon.

....

7. That was the only thing *that we could do.*

....

8. It is necessary *that they should speak* a foreign language.

....

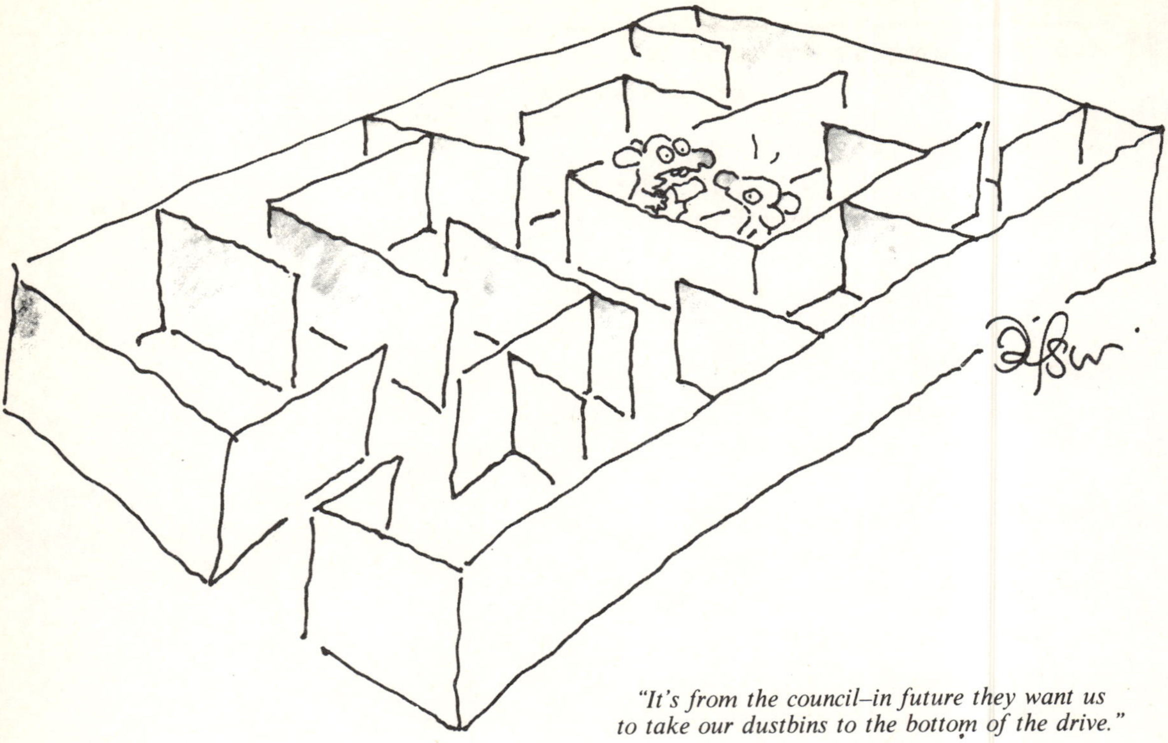

"It's from the council–in future they want us to take our dustbins to the bottom of the drive."

130 ***Transformez les phrases suivantes de manière à utiliser une proposition infinitive (voir A à Z n° 170).***

Ex. : It is important that she should pass her exam.
→ It is important ***for her to pass her exam.***

1. I think it's necessary that I should arrive early.

. . . .

2. He ordered a glass of lemonade so that I could drink.

. . . .

3. Her suitcase was too heavy and she couldn't lift it.

. . . .

4. It was impossible that I should refuse to come.

. . . .

5. It's important that you should read this book.

. . . .

6. Is it possible that you should meet them?

. . . .

7. I brought these hats so that you could wear them.

. . . .

8. It's too cold; we can't swim in the sea.

. . . .

131 ***Mettez les verbes entre parenthèses à l'infinitif passé.***

Ex. : She may (telephone) *while I was in town.*
→ She may ***have telephoned*** *while I was in town.*

1. I should *(thank)* them for their present.
....
....

2. They've already arrived. They must *(leave)* very early.
....
....

3. He can't *(prepare)* the meal; he can't boil an egg!
....
....

4. They may *(forget)* the date of the meeting.
....
....

5. She seems to *(enjoy)* her trip to Weston.
....
....

"You shouldn't have bothered. I could've got a taxi."

6. You should *(tell)* me that you couldn't do the job.
....

7. Their walk must *(be)* very tiring.
....

8. I was so thirsty that I could *(drink)* two pints of water!
....

LA FORME EN "–ING"

A à Z : 174 - 175 - 176 - 299
254 - 203 - 194 - 340 - 165 - 187[1]

132 ***Mettez les verbes entre parenthèses à la forme en "–ING". Attention à l'orthographe.***

Ex. : Bill gave up (smoke). *→ Bill gave up* ***smoking.***

1. Patricia likes *(ski)* very much ....
2. She hates *(go)* to the dentist's ....
3. Do you think it is worth *(see)*? ....
4. Stop *(talk)* to your friend ....
5. What about *(make)* some tea? ....
6. I prefer *(live)* in the country ....
7. Let's start *(work)* ....
8. It's no use *(try)* to run away ....

"I don't swim–but it's handy for washing my money..."

133 ***Mettez les verbes entre parenthèses à la forme qui convient (infinitif avec ou sans "to", ou forme en "-ING").***

Ex. : He told me (start) (look) *for a job at once.*
He told me ***to start looking*** *for a job at once.*

1. We are looking forward to *(meet)* you.

....

2. Let's go now. It's no use *(wait)* for them.

....

3. It isn't worth *(worry)* about; try *(forget)* all that.

....

4. Would you mind *(open)* the window?

....

5. She kept *(come)* back again and again.

....

6. We decided *(take)* the train.

....

7. They told me *(be)* serious but I couldn't help *(laugh).*

....

8. Don't forget *(stick)* a stamp on your letter before *(send)* it.

....

9. I'm not used to *(drink)* so much tea.

....

10. He said he'd like *(see)* the manager.

....

134 ***Choisissez la réponse qui convient.***

1. He's afraid of .... out alone.
   a. *go* b. *going* c. *to go.*
2. They like .... games but they hate .... homework.
   a. *play - do* b. *playing - to do* c. *playing - doing.*
3. Stop .... and start ....
   a. *talking - working* b. *to talk - working* c. *to talk - to work.*
4. Is there anything here worth ....?
   a. *to see* b. *see* c. *seeing.*
5. He taught me how .... the computer.
   a. *to use* b. *use* c. *using.*
6. She looks happy and keeps ....
   a. *to smile* b. *smile* c. *smiling.*
7. Don't forget .... your hands before .... your dinner.
   a. *to wash - having* b. *washing - to have* c. *to wash - to have.*
8. We are not allowed .... here.
   a. *to park* b. *parking* c. *park.*
9. I brought a magazine for ....
   a. *your reading* b. *you read* c. *you to read.*
10. You'd better .... if you want .... your train.
    a. *hurry up - catch* b. *hurrying up - catching* c. *hurry up - to catch.*
11. I got tired of .... for him ....
    a. *waiting - to arrive* b. *wait - arrive* c. *waiting - arriving.*
12. He was not used to .... on the left side of the road.
    a. *drive* b. *have driven* c. *driving.*
13. She hates .... letters.
    a. *to write* b. *writing* c. *write.*
14. They told me .... as early as possible.
    a. *to try to come* b. *trying to come* c. *try come.*
15. Would you like .... in my car?
    a. *come* b. *coming* c. *to come.*
16. The cathedral is worth ....
    a. *to visit* b. *visiting* c. *to be visited.*
17. John makes a living by ....
    a. *teaching* b. *teach* c. *to teach.*
18. Please go on ....; I don't mind ....
    a. *write – wait* b. *writing – to wait* c. *writing – waiting.*
19. It's difficult for me ....
    a. *to understand* b. *understanding* c. *understand.*
20. His doctor told him .... beer.
    a. *give up drink* b. *to give up drinking* c. *giving up to drink.*

L'ORDRE DES MOTS DANS LA PHRASE

A à Z

231 - 232
233 - 298

LA PLACE DES ADVERBES

A à Z : 231 - 232
233 - 298

"May I introduce Cyril who has always wanted to be a writer... Arthur always wanted to be an artist. Lionel had hoped to be a composer..."

135 ***Mettez l'adverbe de fréquence entre parenthèses à la place qui convient.***

Ex. : He went home at five o'clock. (always)
→ *He **always** went home at five o'clock.*

1. Have you been to a foreign country? *(ever)*

....

2. It rains here in April. *(often)*

....

3. We are at home in the evenings. *(usually)*

....

4. I have seen a garden as beautiful as this. *(never)*

....

5. He goes to bed before midnight. *(rarely)*

....

6. The sun rises in the east. *(always)*

....

7. I have letters from them. *(sometimes)*

....

8. Old Mrs Smith goes out now. *(hardly ever)*

....

136 ***Placez l'adverbe entre parenthèses à l'endroit qui convient.***

Ex. : She can speak Italian. (very well)
*She can speak Italian **very well.***

1. I had gone when John arrived. *(already).*

....

2. This dress is as nice as that one. *(just)*

....

3. Do they go to the seaside every summer? *(still)*

....

4. He is very tired; he can walk *(hardly)*

....

5. We have received no letter from Richard. *(yet)*

....

6. There was fog and Patricia was driving. *(carefully)*

....

7. They had eaten corn flakes before. *(never)*

....

8. He carries an umbrella over his arm. *(always)*

....

LA PLACE DES COMPLÉMENTS

A à Z : 231
232 - 233

137 ***Les phrases suivantes ont été coupées en deux parties. Essayez de les reconstituer.***

*Ex. : **1 - c.***

1. She wears	a. a red bicycle?
2. I have never been	b. on Sundays?
3. Do you know	c. really strange clothes.
4. Does he still work	d. writing letters.
5. John doesn't like	e. only a few days ago.
6. Have you got	f. to Germany.
7. The accident occured	g. what they usually say?
8. They've already saved	h. to book your seat.
9. Are you sure	i. a lot of money.
10. Don't forget	j. he'll be on time?

138 ***Les éléments des phrases suivantes ont été malencontreusement mélangés. Sauriez-vous les remettre en ordre?***

Ex. : Walk do to you always work?
*→ **Do you always walk to work?***

1. Liked exercises have doing I never.

....

2. Often neighbour to my London goes.

....

3. Tree under seats are there two the.

....

4. Watch we television evening the usually in.

....

5. Such have seen you ever a thing?

....

6. Shopping went sometimes we together.

....

7. Corner just shop the little is there a round.

....

8. Forget on stamp put envelope to not do a the.

....

9. Daddy last cinema us night took the to.

....

10. Mother medicine my after some takes meals.

....

11. Telephone day other the call from I Peter had a.

....

12. Picture the at page of the top look the at.

....

139 ***Complétez les phrases suivantes à l'aide des compléments proposés (adverbes, groupes nominaux).***

Ex. : He would . . . . . go . . . . (by bus - never - to school)
He would ***never*** *go* ***to school by bus.***

1. I . . . . sleep . . . .
(in a strange bed – always – badly)
2. He had been . . . . waiting . . . .
(outside the theatre – patiently)
3. . . . . John . . . . spends . . . .
(a long time – in front of T.V. – in the evening – usually)
4. I . . . . get . . . .
(by six o'clock – home – usually)
5. He . . . . forgets to put . . . .
(in his camera – often – a new film)
6. . . . . my friends . . . . go . . . .
(abroad – for a holiday – frequently – in winter)
7. . . . . she has . . . . been . . . .
(for a few days – apparently – just – in Paris)
8. . . . . I'm doing . . . .
(something else – actually – this evening).

PRÉPOSITIONS & PARTICULES

A à Z
6 - 35 à 37 - 103[4] - 120 - 124 - 255 à 257

"Never mind–it's good for the swimming-pool."

LES PRÉPOSITIONS

A à Z : 6 - 35 à 37
103[4] - 120 - 124
256[1] - 257 - 340

140 ***Complétez les phrases suivantes avec les prépositions qui conviennent.***

Ex. : Peter is listening . . . . the radio.
*→ Peter is listening **to** the radio.*

1. Stop laughing . . . . me!
2. This is my friend James who's just arrived . . . . London.
3. I'm interested . . . . history.
4. Tomorrow, Patricia will go . . . . school . . . . bus.
5. John is very good . . . . mathematics.
6. We are talking . . . . our plans.
7. I think we'll be back . . . . November 15th.
8. Thank you . . . . inviting us. . . . . your party.
9. *Oliver Twist* is the title . . . . a novel . . . . Dickens.
10. This year we'll be . . . . holiday . . . . September.

141 ***Complétez les phrases suivantes avec FOR ou SINCE.***

*Ex. : I haven't met her . . . . ages – I haven't met her **for** ages.*

1. We've been waiting for you . . . . six o'clock.
2. They've been good friends . . . . they first met.
3. I've been living here . . . . a few years.
4. She hasn't seen Jenny . . . . they left school.
5. His room hasn't been done . . . . weeks!
6. We've been looking for them . . . . three hours.
7. I haven't heard from her . . . . last Monday.
8. She's been afraid of driving . . . . her accident.

142 ***Choisissez la réponse qui convient.***

1. I'm not very good . . . . writing letters.
   a. *in* b. *at* c. *to.*
2. He's afraid . . . . making too many mistakes.
   a. *at* b. *by* c. *of.*
3. It depends . . . . the weather being fine.
   a. *on* b. *of* c. *in.*
4. She said she was tired . . . . working . . . . an office.
   a. *of - in* b. *by - at* c. *at - from.*
5. The road goes . . . . the river . . . . a tunnel.
   a. *over - by* b. *under - through* - c. *across - in.*
6. Don't forget to switch off the light . . . . leaving.
   a. *in* b. *after* c. *before.*
7. John could succeed . . . . working harder.
   a. *by* b. *with* c. *of.*
8. This book belongs . . . . me.
   a. *at* b. *of* c. *to.*
9. It was different . . . . what I had expected.
   a. *for* b. *of* c. *from.*
10. How much did you pay . . . . this dictionary?
    a. *for* b. *of* c. *at.*

143 ***Faites des phrases correctes à l'aide du tableau suivant.***

1. They used to 2. Does she want to 3. We really need to 4. They're looking forward to 5. He is used to 6. I expect to 7. You don't need to 8. Will they be able to	a) go to the seaside b) going to the seaside

144 ***Trouvez les prépositions ou les particules qui doivent suivre le verbe TO GET.***

*Ex. : The thieves got **away** in a stolen car.*

1. You'll get .... trouble if you break that vase.
2. The books are locked up and I can't get .... them.
3. Excuse me, Sir. I get .... at the next stop.
4. We've got to get .... a lot of work today.
5. When did you get .... from the country?
6. John has to get .... very early every morning.
7. I like him and we get .... very well together.
8. I don't know how the story got .... that he was leaving.

145 ***Récrivez chacune des phrases suivantes en remplaçant le complément en italique par un pronom.***

Ex. : I hope he'll bring back my book *tomorrow.*
*→ I hope he'll bring **it** back tomorrow.*

1. You can take off *your sun glasses.*

....

2. The fire brigade put out *the fire.*

....

3. We must talk over *the whole idea.*

....

4. He always throws away *his old clothes.*

....

5. Can you put up *Mary* next Friday night?

....

6. Turn on *the water,* please.

....

7. She was looking for *her handbag.*

....

8. He has put aside *his work.*

....

---

146 ***Dans les phrases suivantes, remplacez les expressions en italique par des verbes choisis dans cette liste. Mettez-les aux temps et aux formes qui conviennent.***

LET IN - LOOK OUT - RING UP - LOOK AFTER - GIVE UP - WORK OUT - MAKE UP - HOLD UP.

1. I'll *telephone* the station to know when the train leaves.

....

2. They didn't *allow* my friends *to enter.*

....

3. I'm sorry I'm late – I got *delayed* by a traffic jam.

....

4. He can't *calculate* how much money should be left.

....

5. She's very good at *inventing* stories for children.

....

6. *Be careful!* The ladder is falling!

....

7. She is paid to *take care of* the children.

....

8. It's silly to *abandon* studying Italian after only one year!

....

CORRIGÉS

LES AUXILIAIRES "BE", "HAVE" & "DO".

"BE" ou "HAVE"? (p. 4)

1. 1. is - are. -2. is - has. -3. has -is -is. -4. are. -5. are - have. -6. is. -7. have -have. -8. is - is - is - has.

2. When Grandpa was young, he had a big red car. One day, he was driving in the country when his attention was drawn by a cow running in a field. He had not seen that two young ladies were riding their bicycles a few yards ahead of his car! When he saw them, it was almost too late. He managed to avoid them. One of the young ladies was frightened and fell off her bicycle. Grandpa stopped his car and helped her. She was very pretty. Her name was Sarah. You know her. She was here yesterday. She is my grandmother!

RÉPONSES COURTES (p. 5)

3. 1. No I don't. -2. Yes I am. -3. Yes he is. -4. Yes I have. -5. Yes, I did. -6. Yes he was. -7. No I hadn't. -8. No, they weren't.

REPRISE AVEC "DO". (p. 6)

4. 1. did. -2. did. -3. does. -4. do. -5. does. -6. do. -7. did. -8. do.

"DO", AUXILIAIRE OPÉRATEUR. (p. 6)

5. 1. Did they buy this big house? They didn't buy this big house.
2. Does Mary live in Manchester? Mary doesn't live in Manchester.
3. Do they have cornflakes for breakfast? They don't have cornflakes for breakfast.
4. Did Bill go to school yesterday? Bill didn't go to school yesterday.
5. Does Mr Johnson work in London? Mr Johnson doesn't work in London.

"DO" & LA FORME D'INSISTANCE. (p. 7)

6. 1. Jennifer did look sad. -2. I do love swimming in the sea. -3. Bob does want to go now! -4. That's exactly what he did say. -5. Please, do sit down! -6. Do tell me who she is. -7. He did promise me not to repeat it. -8. I did read it. -9. My mother does play the piano. -10. I do think you should write to him.

LES AUXILIAIRES MODAUX.

CAN, COULD & BE ABLE TO: LA CAPACITÉ. (p. 8)

7. 1. can't. -2. could. -3. can't. -4. couldn't. -5. can. -6. could. -7. couldn't. -8. can.

8. 1. No, we won't be able to come to your birthday party. -2. Yes, I was able to meet Mr Smith (him) this morning -3. Yes, Bob (he) has been able to do his homework (it). -4. No, they won't be able to go to Scotland next summer. -5. Yes, she was able to answer the question (it). -6. No, he won't be able to open the door. -7. No, they aren't able to speak Italian. -8. Yes, he was able to pay for the dinner (it).

CAN, COULD, MAY & BE ALLOWED TO: LA PERMISSION. (p. 9)

9. 1. Can I borrow your pen? / Could I ... -2. Can we watch TV tonight? / Could we... -3. Can you tell me the way to the Post Office? / Could you... -4. Can I speak to Tom? / Could I ... -5. Can you lend me 50p? / Could you ... -6. Can I use your telephone? / Could I ... -7. Can John come with us to the cinema? / Could John ... -8. Can you pass me the salt? Could you ... /

10. 1. weren't allowed to... -2. aren't allowed to... -3. be allowed to (go fishing)? -4. are allowed. -5. aren't allowed to. 6. wasn't allowed to. -7. aren't allowed to. -8. are allowed; (AZ 45)

MUST, HAVE TO, NEEDN'T & MUSTN'T: LA NÉCESSITÉ. (p. 11)

11. 1. I/You/We must keep left. -2. I/You/We mustn't wait. -3. I/You/We mustn't cycle. -4. I/You/We must go ahead only. -5. I/You/We must give way to traffic on major road. -6. I/You/We must turn left. -7. I/You/We must stop and give way. -8. I/You/We mustn't turn left.

12. 1. has to. -2. Do you have to...? -3. didn't have to. -4. had to. -5. shall/will/'ll have to. -6. don't have to. -7. Do you have to...? -8. had to.

13. 1. They needn't be there before eight o'clock. -2. You needn't call him Sir'. -3. They needn't ask my permission to go to the cinema. -4. Bill needn't take his car. -5. They needn't speak German. -6. You needn't write to us every day. -7. Sheila needn't do her homework now. -8. You needn't come back tomorrow. (AZ 209)

SHOULD & OUGHT TO: LE CONSEIL, L'OBLIGATION MORALE. (p. 12)

14. 1. You should take your coat in case it rains. -2. You should learn your lesson. -3. You shouldn't walk so fast. -4. You shouldn't use a dictionary. -5. You shouldn't laugh at your neighbour. -6. You should send a postcard to your parents. 7. You shouldn't tell her that you know. -8. You should stop talking to your friend.

15. 1. We should park here. -2. You should cut the grass. -3. He should give them a ring from time to time. -4. They should stop driving so fast. -5. Mary should help her sister with her homework. -6. They should be more careful. -7. They should tell the truth. -8. He should send for a doctor.

16. 1. Bob oughtn't to eat cakes. -2. I ought to see a doctor. -3. You ought to leave at once. -4. She ought to turn down the radio. -5. I oughtn't to eat sweets. -6. Jim ought to do his exercise now. -7. We ought to visit Paris. -8. Smoking oughtn't to be allowed. (AZ 239)

MAY, MIGHT, COULD & MUST: L'ÉVENTUALITÉ. (p. 13)

17. 1. You may/might see him if you go now. -2. ...it may/might be dangerous. -3. ...You might have an accident. -4. ...He may/might be at home now. -5. ...Jimmy might come. -6. ...Prices may/might go up. -7. ...we might get good seats. -8. ...I may/might never see you again. (AZ 199)

18. 1. You could send telegrams, couldn't you? -2. You could give them a ring, couldn't you? -3. You could visit them next weekend, couldn't you? -4. You could call them right now, couldn't you? -5. You could go to the post office, couldn't you? -6. I could give you a lift, couldn't you? (AZ 57[3])

19. 1. The Johnsons must be at home. -2. The train must be late. -3. ...He must be in his early thirties. -4. ...I must have seen her on TV. -5. ...It must be your dog. -6. ...He must be asleep. -7. ...They must have arrived. -8. ...She must be ill. (AZ 207 - 208)

SHOULD & WOULD. (p. 15)

20. 1. Would. -2. should. -3. should. -4. Would -5. would. -6. would. -7. Would. -8. should. -9. should. (AZ 74 - 203 - 285)

21. 1. Occasionally, Grandpa would drive his old Ford to visit his friends in town. -2. Grandma would usually stay at home when Grandpa was visiting his friends. -3. Every Wednesday, she would make very good cakes for her grandchildren. -4. Every morning, Grandpa would play the piano for two hours, before lunch. -5. Sometimes, my grandparents would watch television after dinner. -6. Every Saturday afternoon, Grandpa would work in the garden with the radio turned on very loudly. -7. Occasionally, Grandma would read magazines after dinner, instead of watching television. -8. Once a month, they would go to the supermarket to buy all their grocery. (AZ 348)

22. 1. My father woud rather drive to town. -2. John would rather live in the country. -3. I would rather watch television. -4. She would rather have fish. -5. They would rather play football. -6. We would rather listen to classical music. -7. I would rather read a good book. -8. Bill would rather drink water. (AZ 274)

23. 1. If he listens carefully, he should understand everything. -2. If you take this key, you should open that door. -3. If she phones her parents, they should be happy. -4. If you open that drawer, you should find a pair of scissors. -5. If they look this way, they should see the Post Office Tower. -6. If I insert 50p in the machine, I should get a sandwich.

FORMES NÉGATIVES ET INTERROGATIVES

LES FORMES NÉGATIVES. (p. 19)

24. 1. I don't like... -2. You shouldn't drink... -3. She won't be... -4. Bob didn't bring... -5. Little Peter can't read... -6. They weren't... -7. We didn't see... -8. You don't have to do... (AZ 210)

25. 1. Bob has never been abroad. -2. I never watch TV... -3. The shops are never closed on Sundays. -4. You'll never see... 5. We shall never go... -6. I had never heard... -7. He would never be... -8. They never listen... (AZ 232)

26. 1. Neither Patricia nor Richard could do the job. 2. Neither you nor I could have broken that vase. -3. My brother neither sings nor dances very well. -4. That's neither good nor bad. -5. Neither Peter nor John will go... -6. They should drink neither beer nor cider. -7. Neither Ann nor Jenny have heard... -8. Joe speaks neither Italian nor German. (AZ 212)

27. 1. He'll try not to forget that -2. They told me not to repeat it. -3. The police said not to stay here. -4. She asked him not to arrive before 8. -5. They'd like her not to open the window. -6. It's better not to let them know. -7. He advised us not to take the train. -8. I told Tom not to follow me. (AZ 165)

LES FORMES INTERROGATIVES. (p. 21)

28. 1. Did Mary go...? -2. Would he like...? -3. Will Mr Smith arrive...? -4. Does Bob drive..., -5. Can they speak...? -6. Is she going...? -7. Do we have to go...? -8. Had he seen them...? (AZ 271)

29. 1. What is Mary eating? -2. When did she go to bed? -3. Who was late for work? -4. What were they doing? -5. Whose house is it? -6. How will her parents go to Glasgow? -7. Where is John? -8. Why is Patricia running? -9. How long shall we have to wait? 10. How old is Richard's sister? (AZ 271 - 346 - 154)

30. 1. Can't you listen... -2. Isn't Ann... -3. Won't you go... -4. Didn't they enjoy themselves... -5. Couldn't we ask... -6. Doesn't Mrs Smith often go... -7. Haven't they already said... -8. Wouldn't he play... (AZ 211)

31. 1. wasn't it? -2. can't she? -3. doesn't she? -4. haven't you? -5. did they? -6. was he? -7. did he? -8. hasn't she? -9. won't they? -10. didn't he? (AZ 303 - 304)

LE PRÉSENT

LE PRÉSENT SIMPLE. (p. 24)

32. 1. Mr Wilde wants... -2. Richard watches... -3. He tries... -4. She kisses... -5. Bill washes... -6. Patricia always carries... -7. He changes... -8. The teacher gives...

33. 1. They don't agree... / Do they agree...? -2. Ann doesn't live... / Does Ann live...? -3. You don't play... / Do you play...? -4. We don't study... / Do we study...? -5. Bob doesn't have... / Does Bob have...? -6. That butcher doesn't sell... / Does that butcher sell...? -7 The Andersons don't go... / Do the Andersons...? ...go... ? -8. John doesn't walk... / Does John walk...?

LE PRÉSENT PROGRESSIF. (p. 26)

34. 1. Bill is drinking... -2. Where are you going...? -3. Is Bob working now? No, he isn't/he's not working. He's playing records. -4. ...Those cars are going... -5. Why is Ann running? She's trying... -6. You aren't/You're not telling... -7. Why are you carrying...? ...it's raining. -8. We're having... (AZ 313)

35. 1. I don't understand. What do you mean? -2. They are playing football... -3. He is writing... -4. Do you believe...? -5. My father wants... -6. I wish... -7. ...do you prefer? -8. Father is working... (AZ 310^2)

PRÉSENT SIMPLE OU PRÉSENT PROGRESSIF? (p. 27)

36. 1. John is putting on... He is going... -2. I go... I work... -3. What is Mary doing now? She is having... -4. She doesn't like... She prefers... -5. Bill always writes... -6. The children are studying... -7. What is he doing...? I think he is washing... -8. ...He is doing...

37. 1. b. -2. c. -3. c. -4. b. -5. a. -6. a. -7. c. -8. a.

LE PRÉTÉRIT

LE PRÉTÉRIT SIMPLE. (p. 28)

38. 1. Patricia went -2. We took -3. John looked -4. Mr Riley drove -5. I bought -6. The children sang -7. The park closed -8. I walked.

39. 1. Did Tom work...? / Tom didn't work... -2. Did you remember...? / You didn't remember... -3. Did Sheila forget...? Sheila didn't forget... -4. Did they agree...? / They didn't agree... -5. Did Richard bring...? / Richard didn't bring... -6. Did the children do...? / The children didn't do... -7. Did she have...? / She didn't have... -8. Did they finish...? / They didn't finish...

40.

[d]	[t]	[id]
received	worked	waited
played	picked	wanted
loved	looked	
enjoyed	talked	
happened	washed	

LE PRÉTÉRIT PROGRESSIF. (p. 30)

41. 1. It was raining... -2. We were having... -3. Dick was cutting... -4. Mr Smith was reading... -5. Were they watching...? -6. He wasn't doing... -7. You were eating... 8. Mary was playing...

42. 1. We were having tea. -2. She was reading a book. 3. He was calling for help. -4. He was running away. -5. He was trying... -6. I was/we were waiting for the police. -7. She was looking through the window.
-8. He was following the neighbour.

PRÉTÉRIT SIMPLE OU PROGRESSIF? (p. 31)

43. 1. ...I met..., she was going... -2. ...I called... he told... he was painting. -3. As I was coming... a policeman stopped me. -4. ...I was digging..., it began... -5. ...they left, we were working... -6. I was sleeping... the dog woke me up. -7. What were you doing... I rang the doorbell? -8. The sun was shining... we got up. -9. He was trying... he suddenly remembered...

LE "PRESENT PERFECT"

LE "PRESENT PERFECT" SIMPLE. (p. 32)

44. 1. He has not paid... -2. I have bought... -3. She has not finished... -4. Has John cut...? -5. Someone has stolen... -6. They have repaired... -7. Have you seen...? 8. We haven't heard... (AZ 321)

45. 1. I have just seen Patricia. -2. We have just asked him for dinner. -3. The train has just left. -4. They have just given me a ring. -5. Richard has just come back home. -6. An accident has just happened. -7. She has just found her car keys. -8. They have just had breakfast... (AZ 321 - 180)

46. 1. I haven't seen them for three weeks. -2. He hasn't driven a car for ten years! -3. They haven't talked to me for three days. -4. Your haven't written to me for six months. -5. We haven't heard from Bob for two years. -6. She hasn't taken the bus for months. -7. I haven't eaten bacon and eggs for ages! -8. He hasn't met Peter for a fortnight. (AZ 323 R^2 - 120)

47. 1. He hasn't read a paper since last week. -2. We haven't received a letter from them since June 6th. -3. John hasn't come here since the beginning of the month. -4. Bob hasn't caught a fish since we arrived. -5. They haven't visited London since 1982. -6. I haven't ridden a bicycle since I was a boy. -7. She hasn't had lunch at a restaurant since March. -8. We haven't drunk beer since the beginning of the week. (AZ 323 R^2 - 120)

LE "PRESENT PERFECT" PROGRESSIF (p. 35)

48. 1. ...have you been waiting...? -2. They have been living... -3. Richard has been digging... -4. The telephone has been ringing... -5. He has been driving... -6. She has been wearing... -7. The have been watching... -8. Baby has been crying...

49. 1. John, has been sleeping since 10 o'clock. -2. I have been waiting for three hours. -3. He has been working for us since 1980. -4. We have been living in Bristol for five years. -5. She has been fishing for one hour. -6. They have been playing chess since 4 p.m. -7. The sun has been shining for a fortnight. -8. Bill has been reading that book since the beginning of the afternoon.

PRÉTÉRIT OU "PRESENT PERFECT"? (p. 36)

50. 1. b. -2. a. -3. b. -4. c. -5. b. -6. a. -7. c. -8. b. -9. a. -10. b.

51. 1. My neighbours have just bought... -2. We have never been... -3. Peter and I went... -4. Patricia started... -5. We left... and got... -6. She has not/hasn't finished... -7. The Johnsons have lived/have been living... -8. I have waited/have been waiting... -9. ...Jim broke... -10. They arrived...

LE "PLUPERFECT"

LE "PLUPERFECT" SIMPLE. (p. 38)

52. 1. We had heard that strange story before. -2. Mr and Mrs Holden had been in Brussels before. -3. Richard had borrowed my bicycle before. -4. He had given us a little money before. -5. Sheila had had fish and chips before. -6. Bill had driven a big tractor before. -7. The children had brought me flowers before. -8. I had played football with my friends before.

53. 1. It had started raining when I went out. -2. Paul had left for France when his friend came to see him. -3. Ann had had dinner when Peter invited her to go to a restaurant. -4. The play had begun when I arrived at the theatre. -5. We had read the book when we saw the film. -6. John had finished his work when they offered to help him. -7. They had taken all the seats when a woman came in with a baby. -8. The thieves had run away when we called the police.

LE "PLUPERFECT" PROGRESSIF. (p. 40)

54. 1. I'd been looking.../Had I been looking...? / I hadn't been looking... -2. She'd been driving.../Had she been driving...? She hadn't been driving... -3. They'd been dancing.../Had they been dancing...?/They hadn't been dancing... -4. It'd been raining.../Had it been raining...?/It hadn't been raining... -5. He'd been talking.../Had he been talking...?/He hadn't been talking... -6. The wind had been blowing.../Had the wind been blowing...?/The wind hadn't been blowing... -7. We had been singing.../Had we been singing...?/We hadn't been singing... -8. She'd been reading.../Had she been reading...?/She hadn't been reading...

PRÉTÉRIT, "PRESENT PERFECT" OU "PLUPERFECT"? (p. 41)

55. 1. b. -2. c. -3. c. -4. a. -5. b. -6. a. -7. c. -8. c. 9. a. -10. c.

L'IMPÉRATIF & "LET"

L'IMPÉRATIF (p. 42)

56. 1. Certainly. Keep to on your right along Princess Road. Turn into the second street on the right, which is St Cuthbert Street. Go straight ahead into High Street. The Star Hotel is on your left not far from Market Place.
2. (Même réponse qu'au N° 1 jusqu'à « High Street »). When you arrive at Market Place, the Post Office is on your right.
3. Certainly. Keep to your right along Princess Road and take the third street on the right. Go straight ahead.
4. Certainly. Go along Priory Road and take the second street on your right.
5. Certainly. Take Priory Road. Turn left and the City Arms is at the corner of High Street and St Cuthbert Street.

57. 1. Don't listen to them! -2. Wait for me! -3. Show her that picture! -4. Don't take my pen! -5. Switch off the light! -6. Look at those flowers! -7. Don't tell him what I said! -8. Don't go away!

LET (p. 44)

58. 1. Let us go... -2. Let her know... -3. Let me finish... -4. Let them watch... - 5. Let him use... - 6. Let me have... -7. Let us sing... -8. Let her show...

59. 1. Let's have a cup of tea. -2. Let's stay at home... -3. Let's play a few records. -4. Let's buy some sandwiches. -5. Let's go for a walk.

LE FUTUR

WILL & SHALL. (p. 46)

60. 1. ...it will rain/it'll rain... -2. ...Shall I open...? -3. ...he'll be back... -4. ...she won't recognize Tom. -5. I'll have... -6. When will they go...? -7. Shall we have to...? -8. Bill won't catch...

GOING TO. (p. 47)

61. 1. They are going to stay here for a few days. -2. I am going to redecorate my room. -3. What is she going to do? -4. Dick is going to come back as soon as possible. -5. We are going to give you a ring when we arrive in Bath. -6. Are you going to work in Hong-Kong? -7. She is going to buy a new stereo. -8. I am not going to take my exam this year.

LE FUTUR PROGRESSIF. (p. 48)

62. 1. Will you be needing...? -2. We'll be waiting... -3. ...I'll be seeing... -4. ...Mother will be standing... -5. ...you'll be walking... -6. ...she'll be wearing... -7. ...I'll still be having... -8. Dad will be using...

LE FUTUR ANTÉRIEUR. (p. 48)

63. 1. John will have left... -2. I'll have painted... -3. She'll have read... -4. The Millers will have had... -5. He'll have cut... -6. They'll have repaired... -7. I'll have done... -8. They'll have eaten...

LE FUTUR ET LES SUBORDONNÉES DE TEMPS. (p. 49)

64. 1. When he comes back... -2. I'll go on singing... -3. As soon as you learn... -4. We'll have to stay... -5. ...she goes to bed. -6. ...When I tell you. -7. ...I'll buy... -8. ...when he hears.

LE PASSIF

EMPLOI ET FORMATION (p. 50)

65. 1. The garage door has just been painted. -2. Tea will be served... -3. I was told to wait... -4. My watch can't be repaired... -5. Dogs should not be allowed... -6. Bill's car had been stolen. -7. Some smoke could be seen... -8. The instructions must be read...

66. 1. The old house round the corner is being pulled down. -2. Her room was being redecorated. -3. ...You are being watched. -4. A new shopping centre is being built. -5. Bob was still being questioned. -6. The tickets are being collected. -7. The kitchen is being cleaned. -8. The letter was being translated into French.

67. 1. My kitchen window was broken by a child. -2. That big house was built by Peter himself. -3. They are being watched by the police. -4. Be careful! You could be bitten by that dog. -5. Children under 13 won't be admitted by us. -6. « David Copperfield » was written by Charles Dickens. -7. The biggest part of the work is being done by his friends. -8. You have been seen walking in the park by Ann.

LE PASSIF DE "GIVE", "SEND", "SHOW", ETC. (p. 52)

68. 1. I was shown a lot of books/ A lot of books were shown to me. 2. You'll be given a map of London/ A map of London will be given to you. -3. They are taught Latin/ Latin is taught to them. -4. Mary was offered a very nice bunch of flowers/ A very nice bunch of flowers was offered to Mary. -5. Our parents were sent a long letter/ A long letter was sent to our parents. -6. I had been promised a good job/ A good job had been promised to me. -7. He was lent some money/ Some money was lent to him. -8. I was brought a pen and paper/ A pen and paper were brought to me.

LA FORME FRÉQUENTATIVE

USED TO (p. 55)

69. 1. She used to ride a bicycle when she was younger. -2. I used to eat many sweets when I was a little girl. -3. They used to swim everyday when they lived at the seaside. -4. He used to work a lot in the garden when he was younger. -5. I used to live in London when I was a child. -6. She used to practise dancing when she went to school. -7. They used to get up early in those days. -8. She used to wear mini-skirts when she was young.

70. 1. We used to go to the cinema every week. -2. There used to be a big house round the corner. -3. Bill used to drink beer. -4. Richard used to work for Shell. -5. I used to collect postcards when I was a child. -6. There used to be a car park over there. -7. Mother used to tell me a story every evening. -8. We used to walk to school.

"USED TO" OU "BE USED TO + ING"? (p. 56)

71. 1. ...Mr Jenkins used to smoke... -2. There used to be... -3. ...he's not used to driving sports cars. -4. Grandpa used to work... -5. ...I'm used to swimming... -6. ...they are used to having... -7. She used to work... -8. We used to live...

"WOULD" FRÉQUENTATIF (p. 56)

72. 1. Usually he would send... -2. On Sundays they would drink... 3. Every evening my parents would watch TV. -4. Sometimes she would go... -5. Occasionally Peter would write poems. -6. Every week Mother would make... -7. On Saturdays he would have... 8. When you asked her she would give you a lift.

LE PLURIEL DES NOMS

DÉNOMBRABLES ET INDÉNOMBRABLES. (p. 58)

73. Dénombrables: table - cat - house - clock - bottle - sheep - book - idea - man - box.
Indénombrables: milk - money - water - sugar - tea - courage - information.

FORMATION DU PLURIEL. (p. 59)

74. [s]: cups - lakes - maps - parks - coats - pipes.
[z]: apples - shoes - heads - jobs - meals - peas - roads - rooms - planes.
[iz]: places - sandwiches - houses - surprises - offices. (AZ 216)

75.

Singulier	Pluriel
a baby	babies
a leaf	leaves
a knife	knives
a mouse	mice
a passer-by	passers-by
a series	series
a child	children
a tooth	teeth
a potato	potatoes
a wave	waves
a family	families
a brush	brushes
a sheep	sheep
a woman	women
a photo	photos

76. 1. is -2. is -3. are -4. is -5. Is -6. is -7. are. -8. Is. (AZ 215 - 216)

LE GÉNITIF (CAS POSSESSIF)

LE CAS POSSESSIF. (p. 62)

77. 1. It was a two hours' show. -2. It's Ann's handbag. -3. Its a girls' school. -4. It's the doctor's car. -5. Rover is Mr and Mrs Green's dog. -6. It was a fortnight's holiday. -7. It's the goal-keeper's shirt. -8. It's the Head's office.

LE CAS POSSESSIF « INCOMPLET ». (p. 63)

78. 1. It's Mr Jenkins's. -2. It's my sister's. -3. No, they're Bill's; -4. It's my parents'. -5. No, it's Mr Brown's. -6. It's Mr and Mrs Smith's. -7. They're the children's. -8. No, it's Henry's.

LE « DOUBLE POSSESSIF » (p. 63)

79. 1. Patricia is a sister of Jenny's. -2. Bill is wearing a sweater of his brother's. -3. This is probably an idea of John's. -4. I've borrowed a tie of my father's. -5. Isn't it a photo of Mary's? -6. This is a cat of my neighbours. -7. I think it is a book of yours. -8. Peter Jenkins is an uncle of Richard's.

LA TRADUCTION DE « CHEZ » (p. 64)

80. 1. I go to the doctor's. -2. I got it at the butcher's. -3. I bought it at the baker's. -4. You should go to the greengrocer's. -5. I go to the dentist's. -6. You went to the hairdresser's. -7. We can buy food at the grocer's. -8. I go to the chemist's.

L'ADJECTIF

LES ADJECTIFS QUALIFICATIFS. (p. 66)

81. 1. My parents live in a small village. -2. There are tall trees along the streets. -3. I like the old cottage round the corner. -4. There is a lovely park along the river. -5. It is pleasant to have walks there in the evening. -6. The very old church stands on top of a hill. -7. The white building near Market Place is the school/ The school is the white building near Market Place. -8. My parents say they are happy. (AZ 7)

82. 1. I think the book is more interesting than the film. -2. Their house is bigger than mine. -3. Peter has always been better at maths than anyone. -4. He said that cats were more intelligent than dogs. -5. The weather can't be worse than it is today! -6. Mr Simpson is much older than his wife. -7. Her dress is more expensive than Ann's. -8. He has always told us that health was more important than money. (AZ 66)

83. 1. Peter says that Geography is harder than history. -2. Our car is less comfortable than Mr Brown's. -3. I think that things are not as/not so good as they used to be. -4. That bus is as late as usual! -5. Is it true that girls are more sensitive than boys? -6. Your suitcase is not as/not so heavy as I thought it was. -7. This food is better than I expected. -8. I think that John is as clever as his brother. (AZ 66 - 28)

84. 1. The school is the biggest building... -2. The tallest boy in our school... -3. Oxford is the oldest university... -4. She thinks that the most elegant dresses... -5. ...good health is the most important thing. -6. ...here is the latest news. -7. ...Ann is the prettiest girl... -8. That is probably the best book... (AZ 66)

85. 1. Your English is getting better and better. -2. I think my job is getting more and more interesting. -3. Cars are getting more and more comfortable, these days. -4. Don't you think we are going slower and slower? -5. ...money is getting more and more important. -6. He's getting up earlier and earlier. -7. Our house is getting older and older. -8. She opened her eyes wider and wider. (AZ 70)

86. 1. Mr Brown is a broad-shouldered man. -2. John is left-handed. -3. ...She's a broad-minded girl. -4. Richard is a dark-haired boy. -5. Peter is a one-armed man. -6. ...she's a short-sighted woman. -7. ...He was a broken-hearted man. -8. They are good-natured people. (AZ 1 - 8)

LES ADJECTIFS INTERROGATIFS. (p. 71)

87. 1. Which -2. What -3. What -4. What -5. Which -6. What -7. Which -8. What.

88. 1. Whose umbrella is it? -2. What are you looking at? -3. Which boy does she like better? -4. What did you listen to? -5. What is he interested in? -6. What does she look like? 7. Which one will you take? -8. What is it made of?

LES ADJECTIFS POSSESSIFS. (p. 72)

89. 1. your -2. his; their -3. its -4. her -5. my -6. his -7. their -8. his; his

LES ADJECTIFS NUMÉRAUX. (p. 72)

90. 13: thirteen records; 689: six hundred and eighty-nine pounds; 3,523: three thousand, five hundred and twenty-three inhabitants; 3/5: three fifths of a cake / of the cake; 9.81%: nine point eighty-one per cent; 4,790: four thousand, seven hundred and ninety kilos; 10,202: ten thousand, two hundred and two runners: 3.14: three point fourteen centimeters; 1/100,000: one one hundred thousandth scale.

91. 1. nine plus six equals fifteen. -2. five multiplied by twelve equals sixty / twelve fives are sixty. -3. twenty-four divided by three equals eight. -4. forty-three minus twenty-one equals twenty-two.

LES PRONOMS

LES PRONOMS PERSONNELS. (p. 74)

92. 1. Tell her to come immediately. -2. Send it to them. -3. Show it to Richard. -4. Pass it to her. -5. Bring it to me. -6. Lend him some money. -7. Get it for Mother. -8. Tell them the truth.

93. Suddenly Helen started because she had heard a noise in the passage; then it stopped and she knew that there was someone outside the door, listening. She stared at it in a panic. Then she sat on the floor and did not move at all. The man by her side did not move either because he was dead.

LES PRONOMS RÉFLÉCHIS. (p. 75)

94. 1. No, I made it myself. -2. No, the children organized it themselves. -3. No, she taught herself. -4. No, buy it yourself. -5. No, we built it ourselves. -6. No, he writes them himself. -7. No, it opened itself. -8. Yes, we enjoyed ourselves.

LES PRONOMS POSSESSIFS. (p. 76)

95. 1. Bill's car isn't as fast as mine. -2. ...He is a friend of mine. -3. ...Can I borrow yours? -4. ...it's hers. -5. I think Derek is a cousin of his. -6. We were invited by an uncle of ours. -7. ...it is bigger than theirs. -8. My job is more interesting than yours.

LES PRONOMS INTERROGATIFS. (p. 77)

96. 1. What -2. Which -3. Who -4. What -5. What -6. which -7. which 8. who.

LE PRONOM "ONE" COMME SUBSTITUT DU NOM. (p. 77)

97. 1. The red one. -2. Can you lend me one? -3. ...I prefer big red ones. -4. It's a big one. -5. ... - the one with a key in the lock. -6. They think our ideas are good ones. -7. ...as good as Bill's expensive one. -8. There is a right answer and a wrong one.

LES ARTICLES

L'ARTICLE INDÉFINI "A/AN". (p. 78)

98. 1. a; ø -2. ø; a -3. an -4. ø; ø -5. a. -6. ø -7. a; an -8. ø

L'ARTICLE DÉFINI "THE". (p. 79)

99. 1. the; the -2. The; ø -3. The; the -4. ø; the -5. ø; ø -6. ø; the -7. ø; the; ø -8. The; the

"A/AN", "THE" ou ø? (p. 79)

100. 1. The post is one of the most useful public services; it plays an important part in the life of society, both in ø town and in the country. In ø farms which are a long way from a village the postman is a welcome visitor who brings ø news from the rest of the world.

2. One of the most interesting monuments we visited was the Tower of London. Not very far from the City, close to the banks of the river Thames stands an old building which was by turns a fortress, a palace and a prison.
3. One morning, not long ago, I went out for a walk. It was a warm, sunny morning. No wind, just a few very white clouds like ø marks on the blue sky. In the distance I could see a lovely pink cottage.

LES INDÉFINIS DE QUANTITÉ

SOME, ANY, NO, NOT ANY. (p. 80)

101. 1. any; some -2. any -3. some -4. any -5. some -6. any; some -7. some -8. some.

102. 1. There were no stamps... -2. He has no friends... -3. I see you have no pen... -4. ...He has no key. -5. There are no plates... -6. We have no ice-cream. -7. There are no letters... -8. ...There are no seats left... (AZ 219)

LES COMPOSÉS DE "SOME", "ANY", "NO". (p. 81)

103. 1. anybody -2. something -3. anywhere -4. nobody -5. anything 6. somewhere -7. something; nothing -8. Somebody; Nobody

"MUCH" OU "MANY"? (p. 81)

104. 1. much -2. many -3. much -4. Many -5. much -6. much; many -7. many -8. much

LITTLE, A LITTLE, FEW, A FEW. (p. 82)

105. 1. a little -2. a few -3. little -4. a few -5. few -6. a little -7. a little -8. a little

"ALL", "EACH", "EVERY" ET SES COMPOSÉS. (p. 82)

106. 1. a. -2. c. -3. b. -4. a. -5. c. -6. b. -7. c. -8. b. -9. b. 10. b.

ENOUGH. (p. 83)

107. 1. They haven't enough food... -2. Is it hot enough for him...? 3. She's pretty enough... -4. Have you enough money...? 5. He's had enough to eat. -6. Stupidly enough,... -7. John ran quickly enough... -8. This book is easy enough...

LE DIALOGUE

RÉPONSES COURTES. (p. 84)

108. 1. Of course I can. -2. No, they won't. -3. Yes, I do. -4. No, we haven't. -5. Yes, we did. -6. No, they aren't. -7. No, we wouldn't. -8. Of course, he had.

109. 1. Patricia can. -2. I will. -3. Richard has. -4. Mrs Smith did. -5. Jennifer had. -6. John did. -7. Robert would. -8. My brother did.

QUESTION TAGS. (p. 85)

110. 1. were they? -2. can't he? -3. didn't they? -4. doesn't he? 5. shall we? -6. can't she? -7. wasn't he? -8. did you? -9. ain't I? -10. isn't it? -11. didn't she? -12. haven't you? -13. would they? -14. need we? -15. should you? 16. can he? -17 doesn't he? -18. are you? -19. won't they? 20. do we? -21. does it? -22. could you? -23. didn't she? 24. will they?

« MOI AUSSI / MOI NON PLUS ». (p. 86)

111. 1. So is his brother. -2. So have I. -3. So does Patricia. 4. So will you. -5. So would they. -6. So can I. -7. So was she. 8. So had we. (AZ 307[1])

112. 1. You shouldn't either/ Neither should you. -2. We couldn't either/ Neither could we. -3. She won't either/ Neither will she. -4. I'm not either/ Neither am I. -5. We wouldn't either/ Neither would we. -6. You don't either/ Neither do you. -7. She hadn't either/ Neither had she. -8. I don't either/ Neither do I. (AZ 307[2] - 99)

REPRISES AVEC "SO". (p. 87)

113. 1. I don't think so. -2. Well, I'm afraid so. -3. We imagine so. 4. I hope so. -5. I don't suppose so. -6. I think so. -7. No, I don't expect so. -8. Yes, I believe so.

LA SUBORDINATION

PRONOMS ET ADVERBES RELATIFS. (p. 88)

114. 1. which -2. which -3. who -4. which -5. who -6. who 7. who -8. which. (AZ 263 - 265)
115. 1. Here is the key you were looking for. -2. I took all the photos you are looking at. -3. The book I wanted to refer to was not in the library. -4. I like the music you are listening to. -5. This is the kind of story I am interested in. -6. I think you know the people I stayed with. -7. This is the man I gave it to. -8. The chair you are sitting on is an antique. (AZ 263[2] - 258[2])

116. 1. b. -2. c. -3. a. -4. c. -5. c. -6. b. -7. c. -8. b. 9. a. -10. c. (AZ 263 - 264 - 265)

117. 1. however -2. wherever -3. whichever -4. whenever 5. whoever -6. whatever -7. whatever -8. whoever -9. wherever 10. however. (AZ 111)

CONJONCTIONS. (p. 91)

118. 1. c. -2. a. -3. a. -4. c. -5. b. -6. a. -7. c. -8. c. -9. a. 10. a.

119. 1. He spoke slowly so that we could undestand him. -2. I did it because they asked me to do it. -3. You will fail unless you work harder. -4. It began to rain while we were out. -5. The plane took off though the weather was very bad. -6. I'll do it even if it takes me all the morning. -7. She won't go away until you promise to help her. -8. They were angry even though I did my best for them!

120. 1. If I had known where she lived, I'd have visited her. -2. If their car hadn't been being repaired, they wouldn't have taken the train. -3. If it had not been raining, we'd have gone for a walk. -4. If he had sung clearly, we'd have recognized the song. -5. If I had not missed the bus, I wouldn't have been late. -6. If she had spoken French, she would have got the job. -7. If you had looked ill, I'd have sent for a doctor. -8. If he had asked her, she'd have told him the story. (AZ 158[3])

121. 1. he meets -2. we get -3. he is -4. they reached -5. she is 6. you promise -7. he sees -8. I get. (AZ 133)

L'INTERROGATION & L'EXCLAMATION

L'INTERROGATION. (p. 94)

122. 1. How often do you go to London? -2. How long have the Carters been living here? -3. How far is the post office? -4. How high is the Eiffel Tower? -5. How long has Patricia been studying Italian? -6. How tall is Paul? -7. How many pupils are there in your school? -8. How long have you been waiting? (AZ 154 à 157)

123. 1. What is this box made of? -2. What does it depend on? -3. Who is he looking at? -4. What are they interested in? -5. Who is Bob talking to? -6. Where do these people come from? -7. What are you listening to? -8. What is she waiting for? (AZ 258[1])

124. 1. Mr Jenkins asked us who was going to help him. -2. Bill asked me when the next bus was. -3. They asked him how long he had been waiting. -4. John asked if he could speak to Patricia. -5. He asked what the matter was with her. -6. Bob will ask me which one I prefer. -7. She asked how much it cost. -8. Mrs Benson asked me where I thought they would go. (AZ 84)

L'EXCLAMATION. (p. 96)

125. 1. How dirty their house was! -2. How well you look! -3. What a good idea (this is)! -4. What great courage they showed! -5. What a fool Richard is! -6. What a silly book (this is)! -7. What an important decision (it was)! -8. How beautiful the garden was! -9. How kind you were! -10. What a fast driver he is! (AZ 112)

126. 1. Don't they look strange! -2. Wasn't it very surprising! -3. Isn't that noise awful! -4. Isn't it difficult! -5. Aren't they very busy! 6. Wasn't she careful! -7. Isn't it a very common flower! -8. Wasn't that film dull! (AZ 113)

127. 1. The news gave me such a shock! -2. They have been such good friends to me! -3. My neighbours are so nice! 4. It's such a big cake. -5. Bob is so clever! -6. We've had such a good time! -7. I had never seen such a lovely garden! -8. She's such a good pianist! (AZ 290)

L'INFINITIF & LA FORME EN "-ING."

L'INFINITIF. (p. 98)

128. 1. He made me do... -2. Could you tell me... -3. Please let us know... -4. Would you like to come... -5. I'd better leave... -6. We saw them throw... -7. It's difficult for them to understand... -8. His father wants him to be... (AZ 165- 166 - 170 - 187)

129. 1. I was surprised to hear that... -2. It's important for the children to arrive... -3. Have you got a key to open...? -4. ...there was no place to sit. -5. ...the last boy to leave... -6. ...the first man to walk... -7. ...the only thing to do. -8. It is necessary for them to speak... (AZ 122)

130. 1. I think it's necessary for me to arrive early. -2. He ordered a glass of lemonade for me to drink. -3. Her suitcase was too heavy for her to lift. -4. It was impossible for me to refuse to come. -5. It's important for you to read this book. 6. Is it possible for you to meet them? -7. I brought these hats for you to wear. -8. It's too cold for us to swim in the sea. (AZ 170 - 122)

131. 1. I should have thanked... -2. ...They must have left... -3. He can't have prepared... -4. They may have forgotten... -5. She seems to have enjoyed... -6. You should have told me... -7. Their walk must have been... -8. ...I could have drunk... (AZ 167^1 - 168)

LA FORME EN "-ING." (p. 101)

132. 1. skiing -2. going -3. seeing -4. talking -5. making -6. living -7. working -8. trying

133. 1. meeting -2. waiting -3. worrying; to forget -4. opening -5. coming -6. to take -7. to be; laughing -8. to stick; sending -9. drinking -10. to see (AZ 174 - 175 - 176 - 165 - 203 - 340 - 187^2)

134. 1. b. -2. c. -3. a. -4. c. -5. a. -6. c. -7. a. -8. a. 9. c. -10. c. -11. a. -12. c. -13. b. -14. a. -15. c. -16. b. 17. a. -18. c. -19. a. -20. b. (AZ 174 - 175 - 176 - 165 - 299 - 340 - 203 - 187^2 - 103^4)

L'ORDRE DES MOTS DANS LA PHRASE

LA PLACE DES ADVERBES. (p. 104)

135. 1. Have you ever been... -2. It often rains... -3. We are usually at home... -4. I have never seen... -5. He rarely goes to bed... -6. The sun always rises... -7. Sometimes I have... -8. Old Mrs Smith hardly ever goes out now. (AZ 232)

136. 1. I had already gone... -2. This dress is just as nice... -3. Do they still go... -4. ...he can hardly walk. -5. We have received no letter from Richard yet. -6. ...Patricia was driving carefully. -7. They had never eaten... -8. He always carries... (AZ 231 - 232 - 233 - 298)

LA PLACE DES COMPLÉMENTS. (p. 106)

137. 1-c; 2-f; 3-g; 4-b; 5-d; 6-a; 7-e; 8-i; 9-j; 10-h

138. 1. I have never liked doing exercises. -2. My neighbour often goes to London. -3. There are two seats under the tree. -4. We usually watch television in the evening. -5. Have you ever seen such a thing? -6. Sometimes we went/We sometimes went shopping together. -7. There is a little shop round the corner. -8. Do not forget to put a stamp on the envelope. -9. Daddy took us to the cinema last night/ Last night, Daddy... -10. My mother takes some medicine after meals. -11. The other day I had a telephone call from Peter/ I had a telephone call from Peter the other day. -12. Look at the picture at the top of the page.

139. 1. I always sleep badly in a strange bed. -2. He had been patiently waiting outside the theatre. -3. Usually John spends a long time in front of TV in the evening/ John usually spends... -4. I usually get home by six o'clock. -5. He often forgets to put a new film in his camera. -6. In winter my friends frequently go for a holiday abroad. -7. Apparently she has just been in Paris for a few days. -8. Actually I'm doing something else this evening.

PRÉPOSITIONS & PARTICULES

LES PRÉPOSITIONS. (p. 108)

140. 1. at -2. from / in -3. in -4. to; by -5. at -6. about -7. on / by / before / for -8. for; to -9. of; by -10. on; in (AZ 35 - 36 - 37 - 124 - 256[1] - 257)

141. 1. since -2. since -3. for -4. since -5. for -6. for -7. since -8. since (AZ 120)

142. 1. b. -2. c. -3. a. -4. a. -5. b. -6. c. -7. a. -8. c. -9. c. -10. a.

143. 1 - a; 2 - a; 3 - a; 4 - b; 5 - b; 6 - a; 7 - a; 8 - a (AZ 339 - 340)

LES PARTICULES. (p. 110)

144. 1. into -2. at -3. off -4. through -5 back -6. up -7. along -8. about

145. 1. You can take them off. -2. The fire brigade put it out. -3. We must talk it over. -4. He always throw them away. -5. Can you put her up next Friday night? -6. Turn it on, please. -7. She was looking for it. -8. He has put it aside.

146. 1. I'll ring up... -2. They didn't let my friends in. -3. ...I got held up... -4. He can't work out... -5. She's very good at making up... -6. Look out!... -7. She is paid to look after... -8. It's silly to give up...

CORRIGÉS DES JEUX

Jeu (p. 53) : WHAT HAVE THEY DONE?

1. William Shakespeare wrote Hamlet.
Hamlet was written by William Shakespeare.
2. Graham Bell invented the telephone.
The telephone was invented by Graham Bell.
3. James Cook discovered New Zealand.
New Zealand was discovered by James Cook.
4. Leonardo da Vinci painted Mona Lisa.
Mona Lisa was painted by Leonardo da Vinci.
5. Charles Dickens wrote David Copperfield.
David Copperfield was written by Charles Dickens.

Jeu (p. 57) : REMEMBER

Grandpa:

– I used to go to school in Liverpool.
– I used to play football (with my friends, etc.).
– No, I didn't. I used to go swimming.
– Yes, I did. I used to collect postcards.
– I/We used to go to France.
– No, I didn't use to go camping.
– In winter, I/We used to go skiing.

Jeu (p. 61) : CROSSWORDS

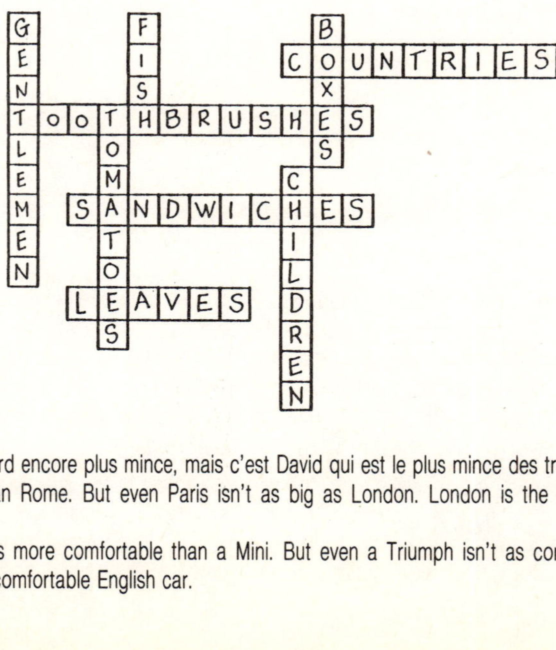

Jeu (p. 73) : LET'S COMPARE

1. Vous avez dessiné John mince, Richard encore plus mince, mais c'est David qui est le plus mince des trois.
2. Rome is big, and Paris is bigger than Rome. But even Paris isn't as big as London. London is the biggest city in Europe.
A Mini is comfortable, and a Triumph is more comfortable than a Mini. But even a Triumph isn't as comfortable as a Rolls Royce. A Rolls Royce is the most comfortable English car.

INDEX

A

A/AN
article indéfini, 98 - 99
a/an *après* what, 125
place avec so, 127

A FEW
a few *et* few, 105

ABLE
be able to, 8

ADJECTIFS
place de l'adjectif qualificatif, 81
adjectifs composés, 86
comparatifs et superlatifs, 82-83-84

ADJECTIFS INTERROGATIFS
What/which/whose..., 87-88

ADJECTIFS POSSESSIFS
my, your, etc, 89

ADVERBES
particules adverbiales, 144
place des adverbes, 135-149
place de often, always, etc, 135
place des adverbes de manière, 136

ALL
all, every *et* each, 106

ALLOW
to be allowed to, 10

ALWAYS
place de always, 135

ANY
any *et* some, 101
any, some, no *et leurs composés,* 103
not ... any *et* no, 102

ARTICLES
l'article indéfini a/an, 98-99
l'article défini the, 99
a/an, the *ou* Ø, 101

AS
as... as, not/so ... as, 83
as soon as *(+ présent au lieu du futur, etc),* 121

AUXILIAIRES
be, have, do, 1-6

AUXILIAIRES MODAUX
can, could, be able to, 7 - 8
can, could, may, be allowed to, 9 - 10
must, have to, needn't, mustn't, 11 - 12 - 13
should *et* ought to, 14 - 15 - 16
may, might, could, must, 17 - 18 - 19
should *et* would, 20 - 21 - 22 - 23

B

BE
be *et* have, 1 - 2
be able to, 8
be allowed to, 10
be used to (+ -ing), 71

BEFORE
pluperfect + before, 52

BY
by + *complément d'agent passif,* 67

C

CAN, COULD
can, could, be able to, 7 - 8
can, could, may *(permission),* 9

CAS POSSESSIF
le cas possessif, 77
le cas possessif « incomplet », 78
le « double possessif », 79
la traduction de « chez », 80

COMPARATIFS
comparatifs des adjectifs, 82 - 83
doubles comparatifs (plus...plus), 85

COMPLÉMENTS
place des compléments 137 - 138 - 139

COMPOSÉS (MOTS)
adjectifs composés, 86
verbes composés, 144 - 145 - 146

CONCORDANCE DES TEMPS
au discours indirect, 124
avec if, 23 - 120 - 121
avec when, while, as soon as, etc. 121

CONDITIONNEL
avec if, 120
should *et* would, 20

CONJONCTIONS
sens, 118
if, 120
emploi des temps après certaines conjonctions 121

COULD
could *et* can, 7 - 8 - 18

D

DÉNOMBRABLES (NOMS)
dénombrables et indénombrables, 73

DEPUIS
for *et* since, 46 - 47 - 141

DEVOIR
must *et* have to, 11 - 12
should *et* ought to, 14 - 15 - 16

DISCOURS INDIRECT
ordre des mots dans les questions indirectes, 124

DO
reprise avec do, 4
do, *auxiliaire opérateur,* 5
do *et la forme d'insistance,* 6

DOUBLES COMPARATIFS
de plus en plus, etc, 85

E

EACH
each *et* every, 106

EITHER
not ... either, 112

ENOUGH
place de enough, 107

EVER
mots composés avec ever, 117

EVERY
every *et* each, 106
composés de every, 106

EXCLAMATIONS
how...! *et* what...! 125
isn't it nice! etc, 126
exclamations avec so *et* such, 127

F

FEW
few *et* a few, 105

FOR
for *et* since, 46 - 47 - 141
for + present perfect, 46

FORMES
forme fréquentative, 69 - 70 - 71 - 72
forme en -ing, 132 - 133 - 134
forme d'insistance, 6
formes négatives et interrogatives, 24 à 31
formes progressives, 34 - 41 - 42 - 48 - 49 - 54 - 62
verbes sans formes progressives, 35

FUTUR
will *et* shall, 60
le futur antérieur, 63
le futur progressif, 62
présent au lieu du futur après when, *etc,* 64

G

GÉNITIF
le cas possessif, 77 - 78 - 79

GÉRONDIF
-ing, 132 - 133 - 134

GOING TO
l'intention avec le futur en going to, 61

H

HAVE
l'auxiliaire have, 1 - 2
have *et* be, 1 - 2
have (got) to, 12
to have + *participe passé (infinitif passé),* 131

HOW
how ...! *et* what...!, 125
questions avec how, 122

HOWEVER
mots composés avec ever, 117

I

IF
if + *conditionnel,* 120
if + *futur,* 119
if + were, 20

IL Y A
Il y a ... que
(present perfect + for/since), 46 - 47

IMPÉRATIF
l'impératif, 56
l'impératif négatif, 57

INDÉNOMBRABLES
indénombrables et dénombrables, 73

INFINITIF
l'infinitif, 128 à 131
l'infinitif négatif, 27
l'infinitif avec ou sans to, 128 - 133
l'infinitif passé 131
la proposition infinitive, 129 - 130

-ING
forme en -ing: 132 à 134
-ing *après certains verbes,* 132
-ing *après certaines expressions,* 134

INTERROGATION
forme interrogative, 28 à 31

INTERRO-NÉGATION
forme interro-négative, 30

J

JUST
just *avec le* present perfect, 45

L

LET
let + *infinitif sans* to, 58
let's, 59

LITTLE, A LITTLE, 105

M

MANY
many *et* much, 104

MAY
may *et* might *(éventualité),* 17

MOI
moi aussi, 111
moi non plus, 112

MUCH
much *et* many, 104

MUST
must *et* mustn't *(nécessité),* 11
must *et* have to, 12
must *(forte probabilité),* 19

N

NEED
needn't *(absence d'obligation),* 13

NÉGATION
formes négatives, 24 à 27

NEITHER
neither am I, *etc.,* 112
neither ... nor, 26

N'EST-CE-PAS?
question-tags, 31 - 110

NEVER, 25

NO
no *et* not any, 101 -102

NOMBRES
adjectifs numéraux, 90 - 91

NOMS
dénombrables et indénombrables, 73
noms avec ou sans pluriel, 76
pluriel des noms, 74 - 75 - 76

NOR
neither... nor, 26

NOT
négation et interro-négation, 24 - 27 - 30
not any *et* no, 101 - 102
not... as/so... as, 83

O

OF
préposition, 140 - 142

ONE(S)
substitut du nom, 97

ORDRE DES MOTS
ordre des mots
dans la phrase, 135 à 139

OUGHT TO, 16

P

PARTICULE (ADVERBIALE)
particule et préposition, 144 à 146
verbes à particule 144 - 146

PASSIF (LE)
formation et emploi, 65 - 66 - 67
passif de give, send, show, *etc.,* 68

PERMISSION (LA)
can, could, may, be allowed to, 9

PLACE...
de a/an *avec* how, so, such, what, 125 - 127
de la particule dans les verbes composés, 145
de la préposition dans les subordonnées relatives 115
des adverbes 135 - 136
des compléments, 137 - 139

PLUPERFECT PROGRESSIF, 54

PLUPERFECT SIMPLE, 52 - 53

PLURIEL DES NOMS
dénombrables et indénombrables, 73
formation du pluriel, 74 - 75 - 76
noms avec ou sans pluriel, 76
prononciation du pluriel, 74

POSSESSIF(S)
adjectifs possessifs, 89
pronoms possessifs, 95
cas possessif, 77 - 78 - 79

POSTPOSITION
voir PARTICULE

PRÉPOSITION
après verbe, adjectif ou nom, 142 - 143
dans les subordonnées relatives, 115
en fin de groupes verbaux, 145
en fin de questions, 123
préposition et particule (verbes composés) 140 - 141 - 142
to + -ing, 143

PRESENT PERFECT PROGRESSIF, 48 - 49

PRESENT PERFECT SIMPLE
present perfect *simple ou progressif,* 50 - 51
emploi, 46 - 47
avec just, 45
et prétérit, 51

PRÉSENT PROGRESSIF
emploi, 35
et présent simple, 36 - 37

PRÉSENT SIMPLE, 32 - 33
dans les subordonnées de temps, 121
et présent progressif, 36 - 37

PRÉTÉRIT PROGRESSIF, 41 - 42
et prétérit simple, 43

PRÉTÉRIT SIMPLE, 38 - 39
prononciation de -ed, 40
et prétérit progressif 43
et present perfect, 51

PRONOMS INTERROGATIFS, 96

PRONOMS PERSONNELS, 92 - 93

PRONOMS POSSESSIFS, 95

PRONOMS RÉFLÉCHIS, 94

PRONOMS RELATIFS
who *et* which, 114
omission du pronom relatif complément, 115
choix du pronom relatif, 116

PRONONCIATION *de* -ed, 40
de -s *final,* 74

PROPOSITION INFINITIVE, 129

PROPOSITIONS RELATIVES, 114 - 115 - 116
place de la préposition, 115

Q

QUESTIONS (LES)
formes interrogatives, 28 - 29
questions indirectes, 124
prépositions en fin de question, 123
questions négatives, 30

QUESTION TAGS, 31 -110

R

RATHER
would rather, 22

RELATIFS voir PRONOMS RELATIFS

RÉPONSES COURTES, 3 - 108 - 109

REPRISE *avec* do, 4

S

SHALL
shall *et* will, 60

SHOULD
should *(conseil),* 14
should *(probabilité moyenne),* 22
should *et* would, 20

SINCE
since *et* for, 46 - 47
present perfect *avec* since, 47

SO
so *et* such, 127
so am I, *etc.,* 111
I think so, *etc.,* 113

SOME
some *et* any, 101 - 102
composés de some *et* any, 103

SUBORDINATION (LA), 114 à 121

SUCH
such *et* so, 127

SUPERLATIF, 84

T

TAGS
question tags, 31 - 110
réponses courtes, 3 - 108 - 109

TEMPS
futur, 60 à 64
pluperfect, 52 à 55
present perfect, 44 à 51
présent, 32 à 37
prétérit, 38 à 43

THE
article défini, 99

TO
infinitif avec ou sans to, 128
to + -ing, 143

U

USED TO
I use to, *etc.,* 69 - 70
to be used to + -ing, 71

V

VERBES
à particule, 144 - 145 - 146
auxiliaires (be, have, do), 1 à 6
auxiliaires modaux, 7 à 23
prépositionnels, 142
sans formes progressives, 35

W

WHAT, 87 - 116

WHICH, 88 - 114

WHO, 114

WILL, 60

WOULD
would *(conditionnel),* 20
would *(sens fréquentatif)* 21 - 72
would rather + *infinitif sans to,* 22

Couverture : Marc HENRY

Illustrations : Pierre FOUILLET

p. 5, p. 16, p. 21, p. 31, p. 43, p. 53, p. 57, p. 64, p. 73

Mise en page : Grégoire BOURDIN

Photocomposition : APS

TABLE DES ILLUSTRATIONS

P. 4 : Dessin de George Mikes, © André Deutsch – **P. 5 :** Telly Savalas, photo © Collection KIPA – **P. 6 :** © 1973, King Features Syndicate – **P. 7 :** © 1988, les Éditions Albert René / Goscinny-Uderzo – **P. 17 :** © News America Syndicate – **P. 27 :** © 1973, King Features Syndicate – **P. 33 :** © Private Eye – **P. 35 :** © Associated Newspapers / Solo Syndication – **P. 38 :** © News America Syndicate – **P. 46 :** dessin © Anthony / D.R. – **P. 49 :** © Associated Newspapers / Solo Syndication – **P. 54 :** © 1973, King Features Syndicate – **P. 68 :** dessin © Ludd / D.R. – **P. 77 :** dessin © D.R. – **P. 78 :** dessin © Roy Nixon / D.R. – **P. 82 :** © News America Syndicate – **P. 83 :** © Associated Newspapers / Solo Syndication – **P. 84 :** © News America Syndicate – **P. 88 :** © 1973, King Features Syndicate – **P. 94 :** © Associated Newspapers / Solo Syndication – **P. 101 :** © Associated Newspapers / Solo Syndication – **P. 102 :** dessin © Ludd / D.R. – **P. 110 :** © Associated Newspapers / Solo Syndication.

Les dessins des pages : 8, 9, 10, 12, 14, 15, 18, 22, 23, 24, 28, 32, 42, 47, 50, 58, 60, 62, 66, 70, 74, 76, 81, 89, 91, 92, 93, 96, 98, 100, 104, 108,
sont reproduits avec l'aimable autorisation de PUNCH

Imp. TARDY QUERCY S.A. Bourges - D.L. Février 1990 - N° d'Ed. 11607 - N° d'imp. 15739

Imprimé en France